This book belongs to

_____

CHRISTMAS GIFTS of GOOD TASTE

ISBN: 0-8487-2430-5
ISSN: 1534-7788
Printed in the United States of America
First Printing 2001

LEISURE ARTS, INC.
EDITORIAL STAFF
Vice President and Editor-at-Large: Anne Van Wagner Childs
Vice President and Editor-in-Chief: Sandra Graham Case
Design Director: Patricia Wallenfang Sowers
Test Kitchen Director/Foods Editor: Celia Fahr Harkey, R.D.
Editorial Director: Susan Frantz Wiles
Publications Director: Kristine Anderson Mertes
Creative Art Director: Gloria Bearden
DESIGN
Designers: Polly Tullis Browning, Diana Sanders Cates, Cherece Athy Cooper, Cyndi Hansen, Danette Martin, Sandra Spotts Ritchie, Billie Steward, Anne Pulliam Stocks, and Linda Diehl Tiano
Executive Assistant: Debra Smith
FOODS
Assistant Foods Editor: Jane Kenner Prather
Foods Copy Editor: Judy Millard
Test Kitchen Home Economists: Pat Coker and Rose Glass Klein
Test Kitchen Coordinator: Nora Faye Taylor
TECHNICAL
Managing Editor: Barbara Marguerite McClintock
Senior Technical Writer: Theresa Hicks Young
Technical Writers: Jennifer Potts Hutchings, Susan McManus Johnson, and Kimberly J. Smith
EDITORIAL
Managing Editor: Linda L. Trimble
Associate Editors: Shelby D. Brewer, Darla Burdette Kelsay, Stacey Robertson Marshall, Suzie Puckett, and Hope Turner
ART
Book/Magazine Graphic Art Director: Diane Thomas
Graphic Artist: Mark R. Potter
Color Technician: Mark Hawkins
Staff Photographer: Russell Ganser
Photography Stylist: Karen Smart Hall

OXMOOR HOUSE, INC.
Editor-in-Chief: Nancy Fitzpatrick Wyatt
Senior Foods Editor: Susan Carlisle Payne
Senior Crafts Editor: Susan Ramey Cleveland
Senior Editor, Copy and Homes: Olivia Kindig Wells
Art Director: James Boone

Christmas Gifts of Good Taste
Editor: Julie Gunter
Crafts Editor: Catherine Corbett Fowler
Assistant Editor: Rebecca C. Dopson
Copy Editor: L. Amanda Owens
Editorial Assistant: Allison Long Lowery
Associate Art Director: Cynthia R. Cooper
Senior Designer: Melissa Jones Clark
Senior Photographer: Jim Bathie
Photographer: Brit Huckabay
Contributing Stylists: Melanie J. Clarke, Virginia R. Cravens
Illustrator: Kelly Davis
Director, Test Kitchens: Elizabeth Tyler Luckett
Assistant Director, Test Kitchens: Julie Christopher
Recipe Editor: Gayle Hays Sadler
Test Kitchens Staff: Jennifer Cofield; Gretchen P. Feldtman, R. D.; David Gallent; Ana Price Kelly; Jan A. Smith
Contributing Test Kitchens Staff: Kathleen Royal Phillips; Kate M. Wheeler, R. D.
Publishing Systems Administrator: Rick Tucker
Director, Production and Distribution: Phillip Lee
Books Production Manager: Theresa L. Beste
Production Assistant: Faye Porter Bonner

WE'RE HERE FOR YOU!
We at Oxmoor House are dedicated to serving you with reliable information that expands your imagination and enriches your life. We welcome your comments and suggestions. Please write us at:

Oxmoor House, Inc.
Editor, *Christmas Gifts of Good Taste*
2100 Lakeshore Drive
Birmingham, Alabama 35209

To order additional publications, call 1-205-877-6560.

For more books to enrich your life, visit
oxmoorhouse.com

CHRISTMAS GIFTS of GOOD TASTE

*O*ver 200 fresh ideas for the holiday season, from delectable recipes to handmade gifts, fill this new volume of Christmas Gifts of Good Taste. Dazzle your family and friends with goodies like Milk Chocolate-Peanut Fudge tucked into jingly felt jester hats, Butterscotch Brownies accompanied by a fancy book for handwritten recipes, or scrumptious Santa Candy tied to a miniature Christmas tree. Each mouthwatering treat is presented with clever keepsake wrapping or packaging so the gift will not soon be forgotten.

Christmas ideas form the core of the book, but there are also projects to help you celebrate New Year's, Easter, the Fourth of July, Thanksgiving, and many other occasions. Most of our recipes and packaging ideas are simple and quick—look for the "easy" symbol at the top of the page.

Let this collection guide you through a joyful holiday season of giving homemade treasures to the ones you love.

The Editors

Oxmoor HOUSE®

Table of Contents

SIPPIN' CIDER

*S*end guests off with clear Christmas balls cleverly filled with spiced cider mix. Just add hot water to the mix, and it's the perfect drink for a chilly winter's night.

APPLE-AND-ORANGE CIDER DRINK MIX

- 1 box (7.4 ounces) dry apple cider mix (box will have 10 [0.74-ounce] packets)
- 1 cup orange-flavored powdered instant breakfast drink
- 1 cup sugar
- 1 package (3 ounces) sparkling white grape gelatin

In a medium bowl, combine apple cider mix, orange-flavored breakfast drink, sugar, and gelatin. Stir until combined. Store in an airtight container. Give with serving instructions.
Yield: about 3 cups drink mix

To serve: Pour 6 ounces boiling water over 1 to 2 tablespoons cider mix; stir until well blended.

CHRISTMAS BALL CONTAINERS

You will need clear, round glass or plastic Christmas ball ornaments; funnel; sheer ribbon; and a hot glue gun.

Three cups of drink mix will fill approximately three 3" dia. glass balls.

1. Carefully remove hanger stoppers in top of ball ornaments. (*Note:* Be sure to use extra care when removing stoppers from

glass balls.) Using funnel, fill each ornament with drink mix. Carefully replace hanger stoppers.
2. Tie lengths of sheer ribbon into bows. Glue one bow to top of each ornament, making sure glue does not cover any part of hanger stopper.

3. Place ornaments in a lined basket or box. Include a note with each ornament telling recipient to remove hanger stopper to pour mix. Be sure to note that once ornaments are filled, weight of drink mix will not allow ornaments to be hung as hanger stoppers will pull out.

CHRISTMAS CHIPS AND SALSA

*R*ed pepper puts the zip in homemade tortilla chips. Pair the chips with a jar of red tomato salsa, saturated with fresh basil flavor. The combination makes great munching food for watching holiday bowl games or old movies. Put it all together in a brown bag decorated with pinecones, raffia, and a colorful paper napkin.

ZIPPY CHIPS

1 package (18.6 ounces) 8-inch flour tortillas
3 tablespoons vegetable oil
¾ teaspoon paprika
¾ teaspoon garlic salt
⅛ to ¼ teaspoon ground red pepper

Preheat oven to 350 degrees. Brush 1 side of each tortilla with oil. In a small bowl, combine paprika, garlic salt, and red pepper. Sprinkle spice mixture evenly over oiled side of each tortilla. Cut each tortilla into 8 wedges. Place wedges in a single layer on ungreased baking sheets. Bake 10 to 12 minutes or until chips are crisp and golden brown. Transfer to wire racks to cool. Store in an airtight container. Serve with Zesty Salsa.
Yield: about 12 cups chips

ZESTY SALSA

3 cups chopped fresh tomatoes, seeded and drained (about 1½ pounds)
⅓ cup chopped onion
2 tablespoons freshly squeezed lemon juice
2 tablespoons vegetable oil

2 tablespoons finely chopped fresh basil leaves
3 cloves garlic, minced
1 tablespoon chopped jalapeño pepper
½ teaspoon salt
¼ teaspoon ground black pepper

In a medium bowl, combine tomatoes, onion, lemon juice, oil, basil, garlic, jalapeño pepper, salt, and black pepper. Cover and chill 2 hours to let flavors blend. Store in an airtight container in refrigerator. Serve with Zippy Chips.
Yield: about 3½ cups salsa

NAPKIN BAG

You will need spray adhesive, white card stock, decorative paper napkins, hot glue gun, gift bag (we used a 7" x 10" brown bag with handles), several 24" lengths of raffia, one or two small pinecones, and decorative tissue paper.

1. Apply spray adhesive to card stock. Smooth printed ply of one napkin onto card stock. Arrange and hot glue napkin-covered card stock on bag; trim edges even with bag.
2. Tie raffia into a bow. Hot glue bow at top center of bag. Hot glue pinecone to bow knot. Wrap gift in tissue paper and place in bag.
3. Tie remainder of napkins with raffia and hot glue pinecone at bow to give with gift.

SCENTED WITH CINNAMON

Cinnamon lovers go crazy over these sweet-smelling ornaments. They're the ideal package topper for this yummy biscuit-based coffee ring.

NUTTY ORANGE RING

- ½ cup firmly packed brown sugar
- 3 tablespoons plus 1 teaspoon orange gelatin (half of a 3-ounce package)
- ¾ teaspoon ground cinnamon
- 2 cans (7.5 ounces each) refrigerated biscuits (10 biscuits each)
- ¼ cup plus 1 tablespoon butter or margarine, melted
- ½ cup finely chopped pecans

Preheat oven to 425 degrees. Combine brown sugar, gelatin, and cinnamon in a flat dish. Dip each biscuit into melted butter and then into gelatin mixture. Roll in pecans.

Overlapping dipped biscuits, place 14 biscuits in a ring around edge of a greased 9-inch round cake pan. Make a second ring inside the first with remaining 6 biscuits. Sprinkle any remaining gelatin mixture and pecans on top. Bake 12 to 14 minutes or until golden brown. Serve warm.
Yield: about 8 to 10 servings

CINNAMON ORNAMENT-EMBELLISHED BOX

You will need two 1.9 ounce bottles of ground cinnamon, ½ to ¾ cup applesauce, rolling pin, waxed paper, cookie cutters in desired shapes, drinking straw, gold paint pen, ¼"w red satin

ribbon, 1½"w red wire-edged ribbon, 10" to 12" dia. round papier-mâché box, and red tissue paper.

1. To make ornaments, pour cinnamon in bowl, reserving small amount to use later. Add applesauce, a little at a time, mixing with your hands until a stiff dough forms. With reserved cinnamon, coat rolling pin and lightly sprinkle cinnamon on sheet of waxed paper. Roll out dough on waxed paper to approximately ¼" thickness. Use cookie cutters to cut out ornaments. Using one end of straw, make hole near top of

each ornament. Remove ornaments from waxed paper and dry on cookie sheet for several days, turning ornaments over occasionally. Once ornaments have dried completely, use gold paint pen to add designs, Christmas wishes, or names to front of ornaments. Allow paint to dry. Tie length of satin ribbon through hole in top of each ornament for hanger.
2. Tie satin ribbon and wire-edged ribbon to box lid as desired, threading several ornaments onto ribbon. Line bottom of box with red tissue paper. Set baking pan containing Nutty Orange Ring inside box.

GOURMET INDULGENCE

*D*elight a connoisseur of
fine foods with a jar of tangy
delicacies. An easy-to-mix marinade
created with herbs and peppercorns
adds robust flavor to Pickled
Mushrooms. Top the jar with
handmade paper and gold-rubbed
leaves; then finish with sheer ribbon
and faux mushrooms for a pretty
presentation.

PICKLED MUSHROOMS

    3 packages (8 ounces each) fresh
         mushrooms
    2 cups white vinegar
    2 cups water
    2 tablespoons vegetable oil
    4 cloves garlic, minced
    2 tablespoons dried minced onion
    1 tablespoon lemon pepper
    1 tablespoon red peppercorns
    2 teaspoons salt
    1 teaspoon dried Italian herb
         seasoning

Place mushrooms in a 1-gallon nonmetal container with lid. In a medium bowl,
combine vinegar, water, oil, garlic, onion,
lemon pepper, peppercorns, salt, and
Italian seasoning. Pour mixture over
mushrooms; stir to coat mushrooms. Cover
and chill 5 days to let flavors blend. Give gift
with instructions to store in refrigerator.
Yield: about 2½ pints

MUSHROOM JAR LID TOPPER

You will need a jar with lid, handmade
paper, rubber band, 2½"w sheer wired
ribbon, gold Rub 'n Buff™, three silk
leaves, hot glue gun, and two artificial
mushrooms.

1. Remove lid from jar. Draw around lid
on wrong side of paper. Cut out circle 2½"
outside drawn line.
2. Place gift in jar; replace lid.
3. Center paper circle over lid; secure with
rubber band. Measure around lid; add
17". Cut a length from ribbon the
determined measurement. Tie ribbon into
a bow around lid, covering rubber band.
4. Follow manufacturer's instructions to
apply Rub 'n Buff to tops of leaves; allow
to dry. Glue stems of leaves to center of
bow; glue mushrooms to stems.

11

RUDOLPH'S DESSERT

*R*udolph's namesake cupcakes draw rave reviews from kids of all ages.
Creamy peanut butter dresses up a dark devil's food batter, as well as the vanilla frosting.
Candy pieces and pretzels make decorating simple and fun. And an easy-to-assemble
sled delivers the bounty.

REINDEER CUPCAKES

CUPCAKES
- 1 package (18¼ ounces) devil's food cake mix
- 3 eggs
- 1 cup water
- ½ cup smooth peanut butter
- ¼ cup vegetable oil

FROSTING
- 1 container (16 ounces) vanilla ready-to-spread frosting
- ½ cup smooth peanut butter
  Large pretzel twists, red candy-coated chocolate pieces, and brown candy-coated mini chocolate pieces to decorate

Preheat oven to 350 degrees. In a large bowl, combine cake mix, eggs, water, peanut butter, and oil. Beat 2 minutes or until smooth. Fill paper-lined muffin cups two-thirds full. Bake 18 to 20 minutes or until toothpick inserted in center of cupcake comes out clean. Remove from pan and cool on a wire rack.

In a medium bowl, combine frosting and peanut butter; stir until well blended. Spread frosting onto cooled cupcakes. Break pretzels into pieces to resemble antlers. Decorate cupcakes with pretzel pieces for antlers, red candies for noses, and chocolate candies for eyes. Store in an airtight container.
Yield: 24 cupcakes

SLED TRAY

You will need four 2" x 18" x ⅜" pine wood strips, wood glue, an approximately 9" x 12" wooden tray, red and silver metallic acrylic paint, paintbrushes, 20 medium silver jingle bells, 2 yds. of leather lacing, small saw, and a hot glue gun.

Use wood glue for all gluing unless otherwise indicated. Allow glue and paint to dry after each application.

1. For supports, cut two wood strips equal to width of tray. Glue one strip to each short end of bottom of tray, flush with edges. Paint tray and supports red.

2. For blades, measure and mark remaining two wood strips 3" in from each end. Draw a diagonal line from each corner to adjacent 3" mark (Fig. 1). Using saw and cutting along diagonal lines, cut off triangular ends. Paint blades silver. Glue blades to bottom of tray at supports.

3. String jingle bells onto leather lacing, positioning jingle bells approximately every 1½" to 2". Referring to photo and using hot glue, glue looping jingle bell garland to sides of tray.

Fig. 1

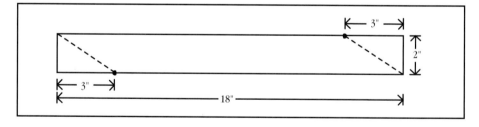

JUST BECAUSE

*Y*ou don't always need a special occasion to show someone you care. Pop in anytime and surprise a friend with a batch of Chocolate Chip-Toffee Scones. It's a snap to paint colorful designs on a clay saucer for delivery.

CHOCOLATE CHIP-TOFFEE SCONES

3¼ cups all-purpose flour
 ½   cup firmly packed brown sugar
 1   tablespoon baking powder
 ¼   teaspoon salt
 1   cup semisweet chocolate mini chips
 ½   cup slivered almonds, toasted and chopped
 ½   cup almond brickle chips
 1   teaspoon almond extract
 2   cups whipping cream, whipped
 1   egg, slightly beaten
     Granulated sugar

Preheat oven to 375 degrees. In a large bowl, combine flour, brown sugar, baking powder, and salt. Stir in chocolate chips, almonds, and brickle chips. Stir almond extract into whipped cream. Fold into dry mixture until well blended. Turn onto a lightly floured surface and knead about 2 minutes. Divide dough in half. Shape each half into an 8-inch-diameter circle on a greased baking sheet. Make cuts through bread to form 8 wedges, leaving wedges together. Brush dough with egg and sprinkle with granulated sugar. Bake about 20 to 25 minutes or until golden brown. Serve warm or cool and store in an airtight container.
Yield: 2 rounds, 8 scones each

PAINTED CLAY SAUCER

You will need a 10" dia. clay saucer; spray primer; green, red, yellow, and blue acrylic paint; paintbrushes; foam paintbrush; water-based polyurethane clear varnish; photocopy of tag design (page 151) on yellow card stock; black permanent fine-point marker; and a glass plate.

Allow primer, paint, and varnish to dry after each application. For decorative use only; line painted saucer with pieplate to hold food.

1. Apply primer to entire saucer. Paint entire saucer green.

2. Use a paintbrush and a stamping motion to paint a ½"w red ring around outer edge of saucer bottom. Paint yellow dots along rim and a 1"w ring of dots inside red ring. Paint ⅜"w blue vertical stripes evenly around sides of saucer. Paint blue lines across bottom of saucer inside yellow dot ring. Paint thin red lines across blue lines.
3. Use foam brush to apply two to three coats of varnish to saucer.
4. Cut out tag. Use marker to write message on tag. Place gift on glass plate. Place plate in saucer.

TOFFEE TIDINGS

A new twist on an old Christmas favorite, our Macadamia Nut Toffee is a dreamy treat for your favorite sweetie! Make it a gift to remember by delivering the homemade candy in a cross-stitched Santa bag.

MACADAMIA NUT TOFFEE

- ¾ cup butter
- 1 cup sugar
- ⅓ cup water
- 1 tablespoon light corn syrup
- 1 teaspoon vanilla extract
- 1 package (6 ounces) semisweet chocolate chips
- ½ cup chopped macadamia nuts

Line a baking sheet with aluminum foil; grease foil. Butter sides of a very heavy large saucepan. Combine butter, sugar, water, and corn syrup. Stirring constantly, cook over medium-low heat until sugar dissolves. Using a pastry brush dipped in hot water, wash down any sugar crystals on sides of pan.

Attach a candy thermometer to pan, making sure thermometer does not touch bottom of pan. Increase heat to medium and bring to a boil. Cook, without stirring, until mixture reaches hard-crack stage (approximately 300 to 310 degrees). Test about ½ teaspoon mixture in ice water. Mixture will form brittle threads in ice water and will remain brittle when removed from water.

Remove from heat and stir in vanilla. Spread mixture into prepared pan. Sprinkle chocolate chips over hot candy; spread melted chocolate with a knife. Sprinkle macadamia nuts over melted

chocolate; press into chocolate. Chill 1 hour or until chocolate hardens.

Break toffee into pieces. Store in an airtight container in a cool place.
Yield: about 1¼ pounds candy

CROSS-STITCHED SANTA BAG

You will need white Aida (14 ct), embroidery floss (see color key, page 133), small bakery box, and 21" of ⅝"w satin ribbon.

Refer to Cross Stitch, page 154, before beginning project.

1. Cut a 7¾" x 13¾" piece of Aida. Using three strands of floss for *Cross Stitches* and one strand of floss for *Backstitches* and *French Knots,* stitch design, page 133, on Aida, with bottom of design 2½" from one short edge.

2. Trim 1" from all sides of stitched piece. Cut a piece of Aida the same size as stitched piece for back of bag.

3. Matching right sides of Aida pieces and using a ½" seam allowance, stitch sides and bottom of bag. Follow Steps 3, 4, and 5 of *Making a Fabric Bag,* page 154, to make bag with flat bottom and to hem top edges of bag. Place candy in box; place box in bag. Tie ribbon into a bow around top of bag.

LUSCIOUS LIQUEUR

Make this velvety smooth chocolate liqueur well in advance of the holiday season. It's infused with fresh mint for a cool flavor that complements chocolate perfectly. Nestle a bottle of liqueur in a basket along with a pair of snowmen mugs for a special gift.

CHOCOLATE-MINT LIQUEUR

⅔ cup Dutch process cocoa
½ cup crème de cacao
4 cups vodka
¾ cup fresh mint leaves, crushed
1 cup sugar
½ cup water

In a large nonmetal container, stir cocoa and crème de cacao until smooth. Add vodka and mint leaves. Cover and allow to stand at room temperature at least 1 week or up to 4 weeks.

Strain liquid into another nonmetal container. In a small saucepan, combine sugar and water over medium-low heat. Cook until sugar is dissolved. Increase heat to high and bring syrup to a boil; boil 1 minute. Allow syrup to cool. Add sugar syrup to liqueur to desired taste. Serve liqueur as prepared over ice or stir into hot chocolate or coffee.
Yield: about 5½ cups liqueur

SNOWMEN MUGS

For each mug, you will need paper-backed fusible web; 3½" x 10" piece of blue fabric; 3½" x 10" piece of white flannel; scraps of white, red, yellow, green, and bright pink felt; black embroidery floss; embroidery needle; sewing needle and white thread; four orange seed beads; and an insulated craft mug with removable liner.

You will also need a glass flask, blue grosgrain ribbon, natural-colored basket, and excelsior.

1. Cut 3½" x 10" piece of fusible web. Press fusible web piece to wrong side of blue fabric piece. Remove paper backing. Fuse blue fabric piece to white flannel piece.
2. Use patterns, page 132, and follow *Making Appliqués,* page 153, to make four snowmen and five pom-poms from white, one Hat A from red, one Hat B from yellow, one Hat C from green, and one Hat C from bright pink. Remove paper backing.
3. Referring to photo and pattern for placement, use three strands of black embroidery floss to make *French Knot* eyes, page 155, and to make *Running Stitch* mouths on snowmen. Use sewing needle and thread to stitch one orange seed bead in place on each snowman for nose.
4. Centering top to bottom, fuse snowmen to blue background fabric piece, beginning approximately ¾" from each short end and fusing in following order: snowman, hat, and pom-pom.
5. Remove liner from mug. Insert finished snowman panel in mug. Reinsert liner and press tightly in place.
6. Fill flask with Chocolate-Mint Liqueur. Tie blue grosgrain ribbon into a bow around top of flask; tie ribbon into a bow around handles of two mugs. Fill basket with excelsior. Place mugs and flask in basket.

PRETZEL PANACHE

Entice your family and friends with this sinfully gooey snack. The combination of chocolate, caramel, and pecans covering crunchy pretzels is scrumptious—you'll never eat plain pretzels again! Stack the snack in a festive fabric-covered box for gift giving.

CHOCO-CARAMEL-NUT PRETZELS

- 2 packages (14 ounces each) caramels
- ¼ cup water
- 1 package (10 ounces) Bavarian-style hard pretzels
- 1¼ cups finely chopped, toasted pecans
- 1 package (12 ounces) semisweet chocolate chips
- 8 ounces chocolate candy coating

Combine caramels and water in a heavy medium saucepan over medium-low heat. Stirring frequently, cook about 35 minutes or until mixture is smooth. Holding each pretzel with tongs, dip one side into caramel, sprinkle with nuts, and place on waxed paper-lined baking sheet. Chill about 10 minutes or until caramel is set.

Melt chocolate chips and candy coating in a heavy medium saucepan over low heat. Remove from heat. (If chocolate begins to harden, return to heat.) Drizzle chocolate over caramel-coated pretzels. Let stand about 1 hour at room temperature (or 10 minutes in refrigerator) or until chocolate hardens. Store pretzels in an airtight container in a cool place.

Yield: about 30 pretzels

FABRIC-COVERED GIFT BOX AND GIFT TAG

You will need ½ yd. of plaid fabric, liquid ravel preventer, 8" hexagonal papier-mâché box, hot glue gun, 8" square of quilt batting, sewing needle and thread, one 2" half-dome covered button form, large needle, 5" thin flexible wire, wire cutters, 1¾ yd. of ½"w green satin ribbon, round cardboard gift tag, paper-backed fusible web scrap, silver dimensional fabric paint, 12" of ¼"w red satin ribbon, and red shredded paper.

Allow liquid ravel preventer, glue, and paint to dry after each application.

1. To cover box bottom, cut one 7" x 26" piece from plaid fabric. Apply liquid ravel preventer along both long cut edges. Beginning on one flat side of box bottom, attach one long edge of fabric to box with line of glue along top edge of box bottom. (Turn cut short end under slightly before gluing in place.) Turn box bottom upside down. Fold excess fabric at each corner so that fabric lies flat on bottom of box. Glue folds in place at bottom of box. Cut one 4½" dia. circle from plaid fabric. Apply ravel preventer to cut edge of circle. Glue fabric circle over center of box bottom, covering folded fabric ends.

2. To cover box top, cut one 4½" x 26" piece from fabric. Apply ravel preventer along both long cut edges. Glue 8" square of batting to top of box top. Trim excess batting from edges of top. Beginning on one flat side of box top, glue one long edge to box top so that one long edge of fabric is flush with bottom

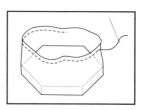

Fig. 1

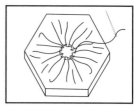

Fig. 2

edge of box top and opposite long edge is sticking up. Use needle and thread to run basting stitch around free edge of fabric (Fig. 1). Pull basting stitches to gather fabric over batting (Fig. 2); secure gathers.

3. Referring to manufacturer's instructions, cover button with plaid fabric. Use large needle to punch two small holes, side by side, in center of box top. Insert wire through shank of covered button. Insert wire ends through holes in center of box top; twist ends together at inside of box to secure. Use wire cutters to clip excess wire. Glue ½"w satin ribbon around outside lip of lid.

4. To make gift tag, using cardboard gift tag as a pattern, trace around tag two times on paper side of fusible web. Roughly cut around circles. Press fusible web circles onto wrong side of plaid fabric. Cut out along pattern lines. Remove paper backing. Fuse one fabric circle to each side of cardboard tag. Use large needle to punch hole in top of tag. Use fabric paint to write name on tag. Thread ¼"w ribbon through hole. Tie tag around button on top of box. FIll box with paper shreds; add gift.

SASSY SPREAD

*S*easoned with green chiles, chopped jalapeño pepper, and taco spice mix, this three-cheese spread heats up holiday fun. Deliver it in this simple holiday bag along with crackers or chips.

MEXICAN CHEESE SPREAD

- 1 package (8 ounces) cream cheese, softened
- 2 cups (8 ounces) shredded combined Colby and Monterey Jack cheese
- ½ cup sour cream
- 4 teaspoons taco seasoning mix
- 2 cans (4½ ounces each) chopped green chiles, drained
- ¼ cup finely chopped green pepper
- ¼ cup finely chopped green onions
- 1 teaspoon finely chopped pickled jalapeño pepper
  Crackers to serve

In a medium bowl, beat cream cheese until fluffy. Add cheese, sour cream, and taco seasoning; beat until well blended. Stir in green chiles, green pepper, green onions, and jalapeño pepper. Transfer to gift container. Cover and chill. Serve with crackers.
Yield: about 3 cups spread

CHILI-STAMPED WHITE BAG

You will need rubber stamps and ink pads (we used "Season's Greetings" and chili-pepper rubber stamps and red and green ink pads), hole punch, 5¼" x 8¼" white paper bag with handles, and 1 yd. of ⅛"w ribbon.

1. Using rubber stamps and ink pads, stamp designs on bag; allow to dry.
2. Place gift in bag. Center and punch two holes 1" apart between handles at top of bag.

3. Cut ribbon in half. Thread ribbon lengths through holes in bag. Tie ribbons together into a bow. Accompany gift with crackers for serving, if desired.

PETITE CHRISTMAS CAKES

*R*ed and green candied cherries dot these tender white cakes with Christmas color. Serve the bite-size cakes at a holiday dessert party or package them as gifts in bakery boxes decorated with trees.

CHRISTMAS PETIT FOURS

CAKE
- 1 package (18¼ ounces) white cake mix
- 1⅓ cups water
- 2 tablespoons vegetable oil
- 3 egg whites
- 2 teaspoons almond extract
- ½ cup chopped red candied cherries
- ½ cup chopped green candied cherries

  Red and green candied cherry slivers to decorate

ICING
- 10 cups sifted powdered sugar
- 1 cup water
- 3 tablespoons light corn syrup
- 1 teaspoon vanilla or almond extract

Preheat oven to 350 degrees. For cake, line bottom of a greased 10½ x 15½-inch jellyroll pan with waxed paper; grease waxed paper. In a large bowl, combine cake mix, water, oil, egg whites, and almond extract. Beat according to package directions. Stir in chopped cherries. Pour batter into prepared pan.

Bake 18 to 22 minutes or until a toothpick inserted in center of cake comes out clean and top is lightly browned. Cool cake in pan 10 minutes. Invert cake onto a wire rack and cool completely. Transfer cake to baking sheet covered with waxed paper. Freeze cake 2 hours or until firm.

Using a serrated knife, cut away sides to straighten. Cut cake into 1¾-inch squares. Place squares 2 inches apart on wire racks with waxed paper underneath.

For icing, combine powdered sugar and remaining ingredients in a large saucepan; cook over low heat, stirring constantly, until smooth. Quickly pour warm icing over cake squares, completely covering top and sides. Spoon up all excess icing; reheat until smooth. (If necessary, add a small amount of water to maintain icing's original consistency.) Continue pouring and reheating icing until all cakes have been iced twice. Decorate each cake with red and green cherry slivers. Let icing harden completely. Trim any excess icing from

bottom edges of each cake square. Store cakes in an airtight container.
Yield: about 40 cakes

CUTOUT CHRISTMAS BOX

You will need a plain white gift box, craft knife and cutting mat, tape, green tissue paper, and 1½"w Christmas plaid ribbon.

1. Trace tree pattern, page 134, onto scrap of paper and cut out. Trace around paper pattern on inside of gift box top and sides as desired. Use craft knife and cutting mat to cut out tree shapes.
2. Tape tissue paper behind designs on inside of box. Fill box with petit fours. Tie ribbon in a bow around box.

BANANA BONANZA

Laced with tangy sweet pineapple and shreds of coconut, these golden muffins serve as a breakfast bread or an anytime snack. Pile them high in a basket lined with a fern-imprinted cloth and share with the neighbors.

TROPICAL BANANA MUFFINS

1   package (6.4 ounces) banana-nut
     muffin mix
1   egg, beaten
1   can (8 ounces) crushed pineapple
     in juice
¼   cup shredded sweetened coconut

Preheat oven to 400 degrees. Line 8 tins (cups) of a muffin pan with paper liners. In a bowl, combine muffin mix, egg, undrained pineapple, and coconut; stir just until blended. Spoon into prepared pan, filling each tin two-thirds full. Bake 18 to 20 minutes or until tops spring back when lightly touched and are lightly browned. Serve warm or cool completely. *Yield:* 8 muffins

LEAF-IMPRINTED BREAD BASKET CLOTH

You will need muslin, needle and thread, white vinegar, two 12" squares of freezer paper, fern fronds or other leaves, and a hammer.

When selecting leaves for imprinting, keep in mind that new growth picked in spring or summer will yield brighter green prints. Be sure to practice imprinting on scraps of muslin before you imprint actual bread basket cloth.

1. Wash, dry, and press muslin. Cut muslin desired size for bread basket cloth, plus 1". (Also cut scraps of muslin for experimenting.) Turn raw edges of bread cloth under ½"; turn edges under again and slipstitch.
2. Pour vinegar in one bowl and water in another bowl. On flat surface, layer one 12" square of freezer paper (waxed side down), fabric (right side up), fern frond, and remaining 12" square of freezer paper (waxed side up). Gently tap hammer over paper-covered fern frond. Remove fabric and soak in vinegar for one minute; rinse in water. Roll fabric in towel to remove excess water; iron dry with moderate heat, ironing over imprint only once or twice.
3. Line bread basket with imprinted cloth and fill with muffins.

MARVELOUS MINCEMEAT

*B*eautiful cakes are meant to be bragged about, and this four-layer delicacy is no exception. When presented on a gold painted plate woven with ribbon, this dessert is elevated to excellence.

MINCEMEAT CAKE

- ½ cup butter or margarine, softened
- ½ cup firmly packed brown sugar
- ¼ cup granulated sugar
- ¼ cup buttermilk
- 1 egg
- 1 teaspoon vanilla extract
- 2 cups all-purpose flour
- 1 teaspoon baking powder
- ¾ teaspoon baking soda
- ⅛ teaspoon salt
- 1 jar (27 ounces) prepared mincemeat, divided
- 1 cup chopped pecans
- 1 package (8 ounces) cream cheese, softened
- 3 cups sifted confectioners sugar
- ¼ teaspoon orange extract
- ¼ teaspoon vanilla extract

Preheat oven to 350 degrees. Grease two 8-inch round cake pans. Line bottoms with waxed paper; grease waxed paper. In a large bowl, cream butter and sugars until fluffy. Add buttermilk, egg, and vanilla; beat until smooth. In a medium bowl, combine flour, baking powder, baking soda, and salt. Add dry ingredients to creamed mixture; beat until well blended. Stir in 1½ cups mincemeat and pecans. Spread into pans.

Bake 24 to 28 minutes or until toothpick inserted in center comes out clean. Cool in pans 5 minutes. Transfer to a wire rack to cool completely.

In a small bowl, combine cream cheese, confectioners sugar, and extracts; beat until smooth. Using a serrated knife, cut 1 layer in half horizontally. Spread ½ cup mincemeat between cut surfaces of layer; place filled layer on a serving plate. Spread half of icing on top of layer. Repeat with remaining cake layer, mincemeat, and icing. Store in an airtight container in refrigerator.
Yield: about 12 servings

CAKE PLATE

You will need a wooden charger, drill with ¼" bit, gold metallic spray paint, non-toxic clear acrylic spray sealer, and 2 yds. of 1⅜"w sheer ribbon.

Be sure to use a non-toxic acrylic sealer. If you are not sure if sealer is non-toxic, place a gold paper doily on plate and then place cake on top of doily. Allow paint and sealer to dry after each application.

1. On outside rim of wooden charger (approximately ½" from edge), measure and mark where you want holes. We used a 13" dia. charger and drilled holes at ¾" and 2¾" intervals (Fig. 1). Drill ¼" holes at marks.
2. Spray paint charger gold; apply second coat of gold spray paint. Spray charger with non-toxic acrylic sealer; apply second coat of sealer.
3. Thread ribbon through holes as in photo. Tie ends of ribbon into a bow on top of charger.

Fig. 1

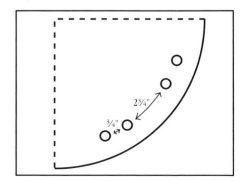

SWEET WREATH

A *wreath of chocolaty,
coconutty, peanut butter bar cookies
is sure to please the sweets lover on
your Christmas list. The bars have
only seven ingredients and a few
simple steps. Present the baked
goodies on a hand-painted mitten
platter that will serve as a fun
holiday piece for years to come.*

CHOCOLATE-NUT BARS

2 cups graham cracker crumbs
½ cup butter or margarine, softened
1½ cups (9 ounces) semisweet
chocolate chips, divided
1 can (14 ounces) sweetened
condensed milk
1 cup (6 ounces) peanut butter
chips
1½ cups flaked coconut
1 cup chopped walnuts

Preheat oven to 350 degrees. Line a
9 x 13-inch baking pan with aluminum
foil, extending foil over ends of pan;
grease foil. Process graham cracker
crumbs and butter in a food processor
until well blended. Press into bottom of
prepared pan. Melt ½ cup chocolate chips
and stir into sweetened condensed milk.
Pour chocolate mixture over crumb mixture,
spreading evenly. Sprinkle peanut butter
chips, remaining 1 cup chocolate chips,
coconut, and walnuts over milk. Press down
chip mixture lightly with a fork. Bake 25 to
30 minutes or until lightly browned. Cool
completely in pan on a wire rack. Lift from
pan using ends of foil. Cut into bars. Store in
an airtight container.
Yield: about 2½ dozen bars

MITTEN PLATTER

You will need typing paper; 13" dia. glass
plate; cellophane tape; red, green, yellow,
and white acrylic paint; paintbrushes;
cotton swab (optional); and clear acrylic
sealer.

*Allow paint and sealer to dry after each
application.*

1. Trace mitten pattern, page 132, seven
times onto typing paper. Cut out mittens.
Referring to photo and spacing paper

mitten patterns evenly, tape patterns to top
of plate. Turn plate over.
2. Referring to photo for colors and using
mitten patterns as guides, paint mitten
cuffs and polka dots on bottom of plate.
(You may find it helpful to use cotton
swabs to make polka dots.)
3. Using mitten patterns as guides, paint
mitten shapes white.
4. Paint coat of acrylic sealer over entire
bottom surface of plate; apply second coat
of sealer to bottom of plate.
5. To clean plate, wash by hand.

FUN WITH FUDGE SAUCE

*P*air hot fudge topping with
its favorite flavor partner: peanut
butter. Friends will appreciate a
gift jar of this thick dessert sauce,
ready to be spooned over ice cream
or pound cake at a moment's
notice. Beaded wire adds an
element of whimsy to the jar and
accompanying scoop.

EASY PEANUT BUTTER-HOT FUDGE SAUCE

1   jar (11¾ ounces) hot fudge
        topping
½ cup smooth peanut butter
¼ cup light corn syrup
¼ cup whipping cream
1   cup chopped peanuts to serve

In a medium microwave-safe bowl,
combine fudge topping, peanut butter,
corn syrup, and whipping cream.
Microwave 2 to 3 minutes on medium-
high power (80%), stirring after each
minute until mixture is smooth and heated
through. Serve warm over ice cream or
cake and sprinkle with chopped peanuts.
Store in an airtight container in
refrigerator.
Yield: about 2½ cups sauce

BEADED ICE-CREAM SCOOP AND JAR

You will need 26-gauge silver wire, multi-
colored 7mm pony beads, wire cutters,
E-6000 glue, metal ice cream scoop (we
used an antique scoop purchased at a tag
sale, but any metal scoop would work
well), and a jelly jar.

Allow glue to dry after each application.

1. For ice-cream scoop, thread one bead
onto wire; loop wire close to bead to
secure. Continue adding beads and
looping wire for desired length. Loop wire
around last bead to secure. Cut wire. Glue
first bead onto base of ice-cream scoop
handle. Wrap remaining beaded wire

length randomly around handle. Glue last
bead in place on handle of scoop.
2. For jar, in same manner as for ice-
cream scoop, thread beads onto wire
length. Glue center of wire length to side
of jar lid at back. Wrap ends of wire
length to front of jar lid and twist around
each other to secure. Bend and twist
free ends.

25

THE ORCHARD'S OFFERING

*S*urprise your relatives with little boxes of lattice-topped petite pies.
*The pies are easy to make using canned fruit, dried cranberries, and gelatin. Weave a
lattice-top crust or be creative and make dough cutouts. Place each pie
in its own little box stamped with apple and pear shapes. Tie two pie
boxes together with holiday ribbon.*

PETITE FRUIT PIES

FILLING
- 1 can (20 ounces) apple slices for pies
- 1 can (15.25 ounces) sliced pears in heavy syrup
- 1 package (3 ounces) cranberry gelatin
- 1 cup sugar
- ¼ cup cornstarch
- 1 package (6 ounces) sweetened dried cranberries
- ¼ cup butter or margarine
- ½ teaspoon apple pie spice
- ¼ teaspoon salt

CRUST
- 2 cups all-purpose flour
- 1 teaspoon salt
- ⅔ cup vegetable shortening
- 5 to 7 tablespoons cold water

Preheat oven to 400 degrees. For filling, drain apple slices and pear slices, reserving syrup. In a heavy large saucepan, combine ¾ cup reserved fruit syrup, gelatin, sugar, and cornstarch. Stirring constantly, cook over medium heat until mixture boils (about 15 minutes). Remove from heat and stir in apple slices, pear slices, cranberries, butter, apple pie spice, and salt until well blended and butter melts. Set aside.

For crust, combine flour and salt in a small bowl. Using a pastry blender or 2 knives, cut in shortening until mixture resembles coarse meal. Sprinkle with water; mix until a soft dough forms. Divide dough in half. Divide one half into 4 equal portions. On a lightly floured surface, use a floured rolling pin to roll out each portion of dough to about a 7-inch circle and transfer to a 4⅜ x 1³⁄₁₆-inch aluminum foil pie pan or other small pie pan.

Roll out remaining dough into a ⅛-inch-thick rectangle. Use a scalloped-edge pastry wheel to cut ½-inch-wide strips of dough. Spoon 1 cup fruit mixture into each pie crust. Place strips on top of fruit mixture; use a sharp knife to trim edge of dough. Crimp edge of dough. Bake 30 to 35 minutes or until crust is golden brown and filling is bubbly. Serve warm.
Yield: 4 pies

POTATO-STAMPED BOXES

You will need a potato; craft knife; gold, yellow-green, and burgundy acrylic paint; paintbrushes; four 6" x 6" x 4" white gift boxes; and 6 yds. of ⅝"w burgundy-and-tan checked ribbon.

Allow paint to dry after each application.

1. Trace apple and pear patterns, page 132, onto scraps of paper; cut out. Cut potato in half. Place one pattern on each potato half and, using pencil, trace around shape. Using craft knife, carve around pattern outline and cut away background to a depth of ¼".
2. Referring to photo for colors, apply paint directly to designs on potato with paintbrush or dip potato into dish of paint as though using a stamp pad. Stamp sides and lid of each box with pear and apple designs. (You may want to practice stamping on a piece of paper before stamping boxes to determine amount of paint and pressure to use.)
3. Dip handle of paintbrush into burgundy paint and then apply dots randomly over surfaces of boxes.
4. Place one pie in each box. Cut ribbon in half. Stack two boxes together; tie one ribbon length into a bow around boxes. Repeat for remaining boxes.

PARTY PUNCH

*P*resent this popular Spanish wine punch, sliced fruit, and club soda in separate capped carafes decorated with ribbon and artificial fruit. Before serving, stir ingredients together—and let the party begin!

SANGRIA

- ½ cup sugar
- 3 tablespoons water
- 1 bottle (750 ml) Burgundy wine
- ⅔ cup orange juice
- ½ cup pineapple juice
- ⅓ cup brandy
- 2½ tablespoons vermouth
- 1½ tablespoons Cointreau
- 1½ tablespoons lemon juice
- 2 tablespoons corn syrup
- ⅔ cup club soda, chilled
  Orange, lemon, and lime slices to serve

In a small saucepan, combine sugar and water over medium heat; stir until sugar dissolves. Increase heat to medium-high and bring to a boil. Stirring constantly, boil 1 minute. Pour syrup into a heat-resistant bowl and allow to cool.

In a 2-quart container, combine wine, orange juice, pineapple juice, brandy, vermouth, Cointreau, lemon juice, and corn syrup; stir until well blended. Cover and chill.
Yield: about nine 6-ounce servings

To serve: Stir in chilled club soda and syrup. Serve with citrus fruit slices over ice.

FRUITED CARAFES

You will need a one-liter acrylic carafe; two half-liter acrylic carafes; miniature artificial oranges, limes, and lemons; artificial leaves; floral tape; 1½ yds. of 1½"w red-and-white checked ribbon; and 3 yds. of ⅝"w red-and-white checked ribbon.

1. For large carafe, select several stems of artificial fruit and several stems of artificial leaves. Holding all stems together as one, wrap stems together with floral tape. Using 1½"w ribbon, tie a multi-looped bow around neck of one-liter carafe. Tuck taped stems behind knot in bow. Fill carafe with wine mixture and syrup.

2. For each small carafe, wrap artificial fruit and leaf stems together as for large carafe. Using ⅝"w ribbon, tie a multi-looped bow around neck of carafe. Tuck taped stems behind bow. Fill one carafe with fruit slices; fill remaining carafe with club soda. (*Note:* If beverage will not be served within 8 hours, consider giving unopened bottle of club soda, rather than pouring club soda into carafe.)

easy!

SQUEEZE THE CITRUS

*T**he holiday season is a great
time to make use of wonderful fresh
citrus. Orange-Molasses Dressing
squeezes the best flavor from
oranges. Just whisk fresh juice with
molasses, mustard, oil, and a few
seasonings; then bottle it and
decorate the bottle with raffia and
dried orange slices.*

ORANGE-MOLASSES DRESSING

1	cup fresh orange juice
½	cup molasses
¼	cup vegetable oil
¼	cup finely chopped onion
2	tablespoons Dijon-style mustard
2	teaspoons grated orange zest
½	teaspoon salt
¼	teaspoon ground black pepper

In a medium bowl, whisk all
ingredients until well blended. Store in an
airtight container in refrigerator. Serve
over salad greens or use as a marinade
for meat.
Yield: about 2 cups dressing

EMBELLISHED BOTTLE

*Dried orange slices can be purchased in
the floral department of most crafts
stores.*

You will need a decorative glass bottle
with stopper, raffia, ice pick or knife,
two dried orange slices, greenery sprig,
artificial red berries, hot glue gun
(optional), funnel, and a purchased gift
tag (optional).

1. Wrap neck of bottle with raffia and tie
off. Using ice pick or knife, punch hole in
each orange slice near edge. Thread
length of raffia through holes in orange
slices. Tie ends of raffia around neck of
bottle. Tuck greenery and artificial berries
in raffia behind orange slices. If needed,
use glue to hold greenery and berries in
place against orange slices. Use a funnel
to fill bottle with Orange-Molasses
Dressing.
2. If desired, write message on purchased
gift tag and tie around neck of bottle with
length of raffia.

MOCHA MADNESS

*W*hen it comes to seasonal sweets, chocolate fudge
may well be the candy of preference. This fudge has sour cream stirred in for smoothness
and coffee granules for that hint of mocha. Packaged in a handsewn felt
Christmas bag, it's a thoughtful gift for family or friends.

MOCHA FUDGE

- 3   cups sugar
- 1   container (8 ounces) sour cream
- 1/3   cup cocoa
- 1/3   cup light corn syrup
- 1/4   cup butter or margarine
- 1   tablespoon instant coffee granules
- 1/4   teaspoon salt
- 2   teaspoons vanilla extract
- 1   cup chopped pecans, toasted

Line a 9-inch square baking pan with aluminum foil, extending foil over ends of pan; grease foil. Butter sides of a heavy large saucepan.

Combine sugar, sour cream, cocoa, corn syrup, butter, coffee granules, and salt in saucepan. Stirring constantly, cook over medium-low heat until sugar dissolves. Using a pastry brush dipped in hot water, wash down any sugar crystals on sides of pan. Attach a candy thermometer to pan, making sure thermometer does not touch bottom of pan. Increase heat to medium and bring to a boil. Cook, without stirring, until mixture reaches soft-ball stage (approximately 234 to 240 degrees). Test about 1/2 teaspoon mixture in ice water. Mixture should easily form a ball in ice water but flatten when held in your hand. Place pan in 2 inches of cold water in sink. Add vanilla; do not stir. Cool to approximately 110 degrees. Remove from sink. Using medium speed of electric mixer, beat 5 to 6 minutes or until fudge thickens and begins to lose its gloss. Stir in pecans. Pour into pan. Cool completely.

Use ends of foil to lift fudge from pan. Cut into 1-inch squares. Store in an airtight container in refrigerator.
Yield: about 5 dozen pieces fudge

PRIMITIVE TREE BAG

You will need a 6" x 18" piece of natural batting; black and red embroidery floss; paper-backed fusible web; green, gold, and brown felt; 10 assorted white buttons; gold corrugated craft cardboard; 1/8" dia. hole punch; hot glue gun; and 12" of black craft wire.

Refer to Embroidery Stitches, page 154, before beginning project.

1. For bag, match short edges and fold batting in half. Starting 1 1/2" below top of bag, use six strands of black floss to work *Running Stitches,* page 155, along side edges of bag to stitch sides of bag together.
2. Use small star, tree, and trunk patterns, page 134, and follow *Making Appliqués,* page 153, to make one small star appliqué from gold felt, one tree appliqué from green felt, and one trunk appliqué from brown felt. Arrange and fuse appliqués on front of bag.
3. Working through front of bag only, use three strands of black floss to work *Running Stitches* to secure edges of tree and trunk. Work several *Straight Stitches,* page 154, around star. Use six strands of red floss to sew one button to center on star and eight buttons on tree.
4. Trace large star pattern onto cardboard; cut out. Punch a hole in one point of star. Glue remaining button to center on corrugated side of star.
5. Place gift in resealable plastic bag; then place gift in felt bag. Gather top of bag; leaving 3" of each end of wire free, loosely twist wire around bag 1 1/2" below top to secure. Thread one end of wire through hole in star. Wrap each wire end around a pencil to curl.

SANTA'S POPCORN

Flavored with cinnamon candies, this sweet-hot popcorn is sure to be a hit with any merry muncher. And who knew bubble wrap could be so crafty? Spray paint it white and use it to decorate a special Santa bag to deliver the homemade gift.

RED HOT POPCORN

32	cups popped popcorn (3 to 4 bags microwave popcorn)
1	cup butter or margarine
2	cups sugar
1	package (9 ounces) small red cinnamon candies
½	cup light corn syrup
1	teaspoon salt
½	teaspoon baking soda
⅛	teaspoon red liquid food coloring

Preheat oven to 250 degrees. Place popcorn in a lightly greased large roasting pan. In a heavy large saucepan, melt butter over medium-high heat. Stir in sugar, cinnamon candies, corn syrup, and salt. Stirring constantly, bring mixture to a boil. Continue stirring and boil 5 minutes or until candies melt. Remove from heat; stir in baking soda and food coloring (mixture will foam). Pour syrup over popcorn; stir until well coated. Bake 45 minutes, stirring every 15 minutes. Spread on lightly greased aluminum foil to cool. Store in an airtight container.
Yield: about 36 cups popcorn

BUBBLE WRAP SANTA BAG

You will need tracing paper; red, pink, black, and green felt; plastic bubble wrap;

Design Master® white spray paint; low-temperature glue gun; 6" x 11" brown paper bag; and a ⅝" dia. red button.

1. Trace patterns, page 135, onto tracing paper; cut out. Using patterns, cut one nose from red felt; two cheeks from pink felt; two eyes from black felt; two holly leaves from green felt; and two pupils, two eyebrows, one mustache, and one small and one large half-circle from bubble wrap. Cut one 2¾" x 13" strip from red felt for hat. Cut one 1¾" x 14" strip from bubble wrap for hatband. Spray paint bubble wrap pieces white; allow to dry.

2. Arrange and glue cheeks, eyes, and eyebrows on bag. Glue pupils to eyes.
3. For beard, cut several 2½" long slits along curved edges of half-circles. Overlapping to sides of bag, glue straight edges of large and then small half-circles along bottom edges of cheeks. Glue mustache to beard; glue nose to mustache.
4. For hat, overlap short ends of hatband 1"; glue. Overlap short ends of hat 1"; glue. Arrange and glue bottom of hat inside top edge of hatband. Glue top edges of hat together. Arrange and glue holly leaves on hat; glue button to holly leaves. Place gift in bag; place hat on top of bag.

ROSY RASPBERRY SAUCE

*T*his black raspberry mustard sauce is three-ingredient easy and takes just minutes to make. And friends and family will delight in receiving a jar of this ruby sauce packaged in a cheery snowman-tagged bag. Suggest serving the sauce over ham or pork, or as a dipping sauce for egg rolls.

RASPBERRY-HONEY MUSTARD SAUCE

  1 jar (12 ounces) seedless black raspberry jam
  ½ cup honey
  ½ cup prepared mustard

In a small saucepan, combine jam, honey, and mustard. Stirring constantly, cook over medium heat until jam melts and sauce is smooth. Store in an airtight container in refrigerator. Serve as a condiment with meat, poultry, or egg rolls. *Yield:* about 2 cups sauce

SNOWMAN TAG AND BAG

You will need a green lunch-size paper bag, paper clip, 1"w grosgrain ribbon, hot glue gun, colored pencils, photocopy of tag design (page 150) on white card stock, and a red permanent fine-point marker.

1. Place gift in bag. Fold top of bag 1" to front twice; paper clip top center of fold to secure.
2. Measure height of front, back, and bottom of bag; add 1". Cut a length of ribbon the determined measurement. Overlapping at fold on front of bag, wrap ribbon around bag; glue to secure. Cut a 15" length from ribbon; tie ribbon into a bow. Glue bow at overlap of ribbon.

3. Use colored pencils to color tag. Use marker to write message on tag. Cut out tag; glue to bag.

CRAZY FOR CANDY CANES

Bake a batch of these simple peppermint-striped sugar cookies. The recipe's simple; just use care when shaping the canes. And for best results, chill the shaped cookies before baking. Then package the cookies in cellophane or resealable plastic bags and tuck them in a homemade burlap bag.

CANDY CANE COOKIES

¼ to ½ cup all-purpose flour
½ teaspoon peppermint extract
1 package (18 ounces) refrigerated
 sugar cookie dough
 Red paste food coloring

Preheat oven to 350 degrees. Knead ¼ cup flour and peppermint extract into cookie dough. Divide cookie dough in half. Knead red food coloring into half of dough, using additional flour as necessary. Divide each half into 5 equal pieces. Cover and chill dough. Roll each piece of dough into a 15-inch-long rope. Place ropes side by side on an ungreased baking sheet, alternating colors. Place waxed paper on top of dough. Using a rolling pin, gently roll dough into a 6 x 20-inch rectangle. Remove waxed paper from top of dough. Using a knife or pizza cutter, cut dough crosswise into ½-inch-wide strips. Shape dough to form candy canes. Chill 10 minutes, if desired. Bake 5 to 7 minutes or until edges are lightly browned. Let cool 30 seconds. Transfer to a wire rack to cool. Store in an airtight container.
Yield: about 34 cookies

CANDY CANE BAG

You will need a disappearing ink fabric marker, ⅔ yd. each of red and white burlap, masking tape, ballpoint pen, thread, ruler, cellophane bag, twist tie, red raffia, red-and-white striped pipe cleaners, and an artificial holly sprig.

Fig. 1

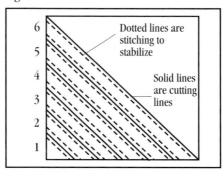

Fig. 2

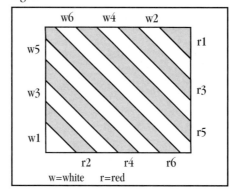

1. Using fabric marker and beginning in one corner, mark six diagonal 3"-wide strips on each piece of burlap. Stitching ⅛" on either side of marked lines, stitch along strips to stabilize (Fig. 1).
2. Place small piece of masking tape on each strip. Writing on masking tape with ballpoint pen, number strips 1–6, with "1" being corner piece and "6" being longest strip. Cut strips apart along marked lines.
3. Alternating colors, lay strips out in red and white pattern to form square (Fig. 2). Using ¼" seam allowance, stitch strips together. Press seams toward red strips.

Fig. 3

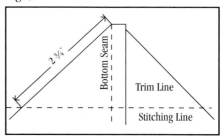

4. Using ruler and fabric marker, mark 17" x 19" rectangle on joined piece. Stitch ⅛" inside marked lines. Cut out rectangle along marked lines. Fold rectangle in half, matching right sides and 19" long edges. To form back seam, stitch along 19" edge, using ¼" seam allowance. Zigzag raw edges if desired. Press seam to one side.
5. To form bottom seam, center back seam and stitch ¼" seam along one short end of bag. To square off bottom of bag, align bottom seam with side fold. Measure and mark 2¾" from tip of one corner along each edge; draw line to connect marks. Stitch along marked line (Fig. 3). Repeat for remaining corner. Trim corners to ½" seam. Zigzag raw edges if desired.
6. To hem top of bag, fold top raw edge under ½"; fold under again and stitch in place. Turn bag right side out.
7. Place cookies in cellophane bag and close with twist tie. Place cellophane bag in burlap bag. Tuck top edge of burlap bag under approximately 3". Tie raffia into a bow around top of burlap bag. Bend two pipe cleaners into candy cane shape. Trim pipe cleaners if necessary. Tuck pipe cleaner candy canes and holly sprig into raffia.

CARIBBEAN CONFECTION

*S*ay *"Happy Holidays" with this luscious banana cake. Both the cake and glaze are laced with dark rum, which adds a bit of island flair. The cake cover, with a string of lights painted right onto the glass, is equally showstopping.*

BANANA-RUM CAKE

CAKE
- ¾ cup butter or margarine, softened
- 1¾ cups firmly packed brown sugar
- 3 eggs
- 1 cup mashed ripe banana (2 bananas)
- ½ cup sour cream
- 2 tablespoons dark rum
- 1 tablespoon vanilla extract
- 2½ cups all-purpose flour
- 2 teaspoons baking powder
- 1 teaspoon baking soda
- 1 teaspoon ground cinnamon
- ½ teaspoon salt

GLAZE
- ¾ cup confectioners sugar
- 2 tablespoons dark rum
- 1 tablespoon butter, melted

Preheat oven to 375 degrees. For cake, cream butter and brown sugar in a large bowl until fluffy. Beat in eggs, 1 at a time, beating well after each addition. Beat in bananas, sour cream, rum, and vanilla. In a medium bowl, combine flour, baking powder, baking soda, cinnamon, and salt. Add dry ingredients to creamed mixture; beat until well blended. Spoon batter into a greased and floured 10-inch tube pan. Bake 45 minutes or until a toothpick inserted near center of cake comes out clean. Cool in pan 10 minutes; remove from pan. Cool completely on a wire rack.

For glaze, combine confectioners sugar, rum, and butter in a small bowl; stir until smooth. Drizzle over cake. Let glaze harden. Store in an airtight container.
Yield: about 12 to 14 servings

CHRISTMAS LIGHTS CAKE COVER

You will need a plain, clear glass domed cake cover; cellophane tape; red, green, blue, yellow, white, and black glass paint; and paintbrushes.

Allow paint to dry after each application.

1. Referring to paint manufacturer's instructions, prepare cake cover for applying glass paint. Trace Christmas lights pattern, page 132, onto scrap of paper and cut out grouping of lights, leaving ½" margin around design.

2. Tape paper pattern to inside of cake cover as guide. Paint lights red, green, blue, or yellow. Use white to paint accent on each light. Reposition pattern on inside of cake cover and continue painting lights around sides of cover.

3. Using small paintbrush and black paint, paint caps of lights and curving "wires" leading from one light to next until all lights are connected in one continuous strand. Follow paint manufacturer's instructions for drying/curing time before using cake cover.

MONSTER COOKIES

These jumbo cookies are loaded with peanut butter candy pieces, oats, and nuts. Use the emptied oats container for packaging. Simply cover it with holiday fabric and fill with cookies.

GIANT PEANUT BUTTER COOKIES

½   cup butter or margarine, softened
1   cup sugar
1   cup plus 2 tablespoons firmly
     packed brown sugar
3   eggs
2   cups peanut butter
¼   teaspoon vanilla extract
¾   teaspoon light corn syrup
4½ cups old-fashioned oats
2   teaspoons baking soda
¼   teaspoon salt
1   cup candy-coated peanut butter
     pieces
1   cup chopped walnuts

Preheat oven to 350 degrees. In a large bowl, cream butter and sugars until fluffy. Add eggs, peanut butter, vanilla, and corn syrup; beat until well blended. Add oats, soda, and salt, stirring well. Stir in candy pieces and walnuts. (Batter will be stiff.) For each cookie, pack dough into a ¼-cup measure; spoon dough onto a lightly greased baking sheet and press into a 3-inch circle. Repeat the procedure with remaining dough, spacing cookies 4 inches apart. Bake 12 to 15 minutes. (Centers of cookies will be slightly soft.) Cool slightly on baking sheets. Transfer cookies to wire racks to cool.
Yield: about 2½ dozen cookies

COOKIE CONTAINERS

For each container, you will need 7" x 13½" piece and 5" dia. circle of Christmas print fabric, an empty oats container, spray adhesive, hot glue gun, and 27½" of ⅜" w coordinating grosgrain ribbon.

1. Fold one short edge of 7" x 13½" fabric piece under ½" and press. Leaving lid on container, spray sides of container and top of lid with spray adhesive. Remove lid from container. Beginning with unpressed short edge of 7" x 13½" fabric piece, carefully attach fabric to outside of container, smoothing fabric as you go. Secure overlapped folded edge with line of hot glue. Center fabric circle on lid and press into spray adhesive, folding edges over edge of lid.
2. Cut length of ribbon so that it will circle lid rim, overlapping slightly. Attach ribbon length to rim of lid with hot glue. Use hot glue to attach remaining ribbon length around base of container, covering raw edge of fabric. Fill container with stack of Giant Peanut Butter Cookies.

CHOCOLATE MUFFIN MAGIC

A basket of these chocolate muffins will no doubt make someone's Christmas merrier. A cross between muffin and bread pudding, this clever dessert is sure to gain rave reviews when served warm from the oven. Give the basket a folksy touch by tucking in a cloth with a gingerbread appliqué and a buttonhole stitched border.

CHOCOLATE BREAD PUDDING MUFFINS

1   can (12 ounces) refrigerated buttermilk biscuits, baked according to package directions
2   cups milk
3   eggs
3   tablespoons butter or margarine, melted
2   teaspoons vanilla extract
¾   cup sugar
¼   cup cocoa
1   cup (6 ounces) semisweet chocolate chips

Preheat oven to 350 degrees. Tear biscuits into small pieces. In a large bowl, stir biscuits and milk; set aside. In a medium bowl, beat eggs, butter, and vanilla until well blended. Add sugar and cocoa; beat until well blended. Stir in chocolate chips. Add chocolate mixture to biscuit mixture; stir until well blended. Let stand 5 minutes. Spoon batter into paper-lined muffin pans, filling each tin three-quarters full. Bake 40 minutes or until a toothpick inserted in center comes out clean. Serve warm.
Yield: about 18 muffins

GINGERBREAD MAN DISH TOWEL

You will need red and black embroidery floss, embroidery needle, green checked dish towel, paper-backed fusible web, red-and-green plaid fabric scrap, cream fabric scrap, brown fabric scrap, and two ⅛" dia. white buttons.

Refer to Embroidery Stitches, page 154, before beginning project.

1. Using six strands of red embroidery floss, *Blanket-Stitch,* page 154, edges of dish towel.
2. Use patterns, page 136, and follow *Making Appliqués,* page 153, to make one brown gingerbread man, one plaid Rectangle A (be sure to pay close attention to grain line arrow on pattern piece so plaid will be cut on bias), and one cream Rectangle B.

3. Remove paper backing from cream rectangle. Center and fuse cream rectangle onto plaid rectangle. Remove paper backing from gingerbread man. Referring to photo, tilt gingerbread man slightly and fuse in place on top of cream rectangle. Fuse entire motif to one corner of dish towel, approximately 1½" from edges.
4. Using three strands of red embroidery floss, *Blanket-Stitch* edges of appliquéd motif, page 154. Using three strands of black embroidery floss, make *Running Stitches,* page 155, along edges of gingerbread man. Use black embroidery floss to make two *French Knot* eyes, page 155. Referring to photo for placement, use red floss to sew buttons onto gingerbread man's tummy. Line a basket with dish towel and fill basket with muffins.

JEWELED JELLY

*Y*our friends will be overjoyed to receive mini totes carrying jars of this jewel-toned jelly. The recipe provides nine jars for gift giving. Use holiday fabric to cover the jar lids and make tree cutouts for the totes.

CRAN-RASPBERRY JELLY

1   jar (48 ounces) cran-raspberry
      juice cocktail
6½ cups sugar
2   pouches (3 ounces each) liquid
      pectin
2   tablespoons fresh lemon juice

In a stock pot, combine juice and sugar; stir until well blended. Stirring constantly over high heat, bring mixture to a full rolling boil. In a small bowl, combine liquid pectin and lemon juice. Add pectin mixture to juice mixture, continuing to stir constantly. Bring to a full rolling boil and boil for 1 minute. Remove mixture from heat. Skim foam off of mixture. Fill prepared jars to within ⅛-inch of tops. Store in refrigerator.
Yield: about 9 half-pints

TOTE BAG AND COVERED JAR

You will need a jelly jar, spray adhesive, two approximately 4½" squares of Christmas print fabric, ¾ yd. of ¼"w red grosgrain ribbon, hot glue gun, scrap of paper-backed fusible web, purchased mini tote bag, thread to match fabric, dimensional fabric paint (optional), needle and thread, red tissue paper, 12" of ¾"w red-and-white checked ribbon, hole punch (optional), and a gift tag.

1. Remove lid from jelly jar. Fill jar with jelly. Lightly spray coat of spray adhesive on top of jelly jar lid. Center one square of fabric, faceup, over jelly jar lid and press fabric onto top of lid. Place lid on jar. Tie grosgrain ribbon into a bow around rim of jar lid. Trim ends. Hold ribbon in place with small dab of hot glue. Set jar aside.
2. Use tree pattern, page 134, and follow *Making Appliqués*, page 153, to make one tree. Remove paper backing.
3. Center and fuse tree shape onto one side of tote bag. Zigzag stitch along edges of shape. Or if you prefer, you may outline edges of shape with coordinating dimensional fabric paint. From remaining scraps of grosgrain ribbon, tie a small bow; using needle and thread, tack bow to top of tree.
4. Line tote bag with tissue paper. Place jelly inside bag. Punch hole in gift tag if necessary. Write recipe name on tag. Thread tag onto checked ribbon. Tie checked ribbon around handle of tote bag.

NO FUSS FUDGE

*E*ven the court jester would fall for this dreamy peanutty fudge. It's rich, so cut it into tiny pieces and stack a baker's dozen in each cellophane bag; then place the bags of fudge into jingly jester hats.

MILK CHOCOLATE-PEANUT FUDGE

- 1 package (11½ ounces) milk chocolate chips
- ½ cup sweetened condensed milk
- 2 cups miniature marshmallows
- ½ cup creamy peanut butter
- 1 teaspoon vanilla extract
- ⅛ teaspoon salt
- 1 cup chopped peanuts

Line a 9-inch square baking pan with aluminum foil, extending foil over 2 sides of pan; grease foil. In a heavy large saucepan, combine chocolate chips, sweetened condensed milk, and marshmallows. Stirring constantly, cook over medium heat until chips and marshmallows melt. Remove from heat. Stir in peanut butter, vanilla, and salt until smooth. Stir in peanuts. Spread into prepared pan. Chill 2 hours or until firm.

Use ends of foil to lift fudge from pan. Cut into 1-inch pieces. Store in an airtight container in refrigerator.

Yield: about 7 dozen pieces fudge

JESTER HATS

For each container, you will need paper-backed fusible web, drawing compass, 6" x 18" piece of Christmas print fabric, 6" x 12" piece of coordinating fabric, 3" dia.

cardboard circle, hot glue gun, five jingle bells, metallic gold thread, cellophane bags, red ribbon, and gift tags.

1. Using jester hat pattern, pages 142 and 143, trace one jester pattern onto paper side of fusible web. Using compass, trace one 2¾" dia. circle onto paper side of fusible web. Leaving margin, cut around fusible web shapes. Press fusible web shapes onto wrong side of 6" x 18" Christmas print fabric piece. Cut out shapes along pattern lines. Remove paper backing from both pieces, except from tab on jester piece. Set circle aside. Fuse jester

piece to 6" x 12" coordinating fabric piece. Trim fabric.

2. Overlap ends of jester piece to form ring, with Christmas print to outside. Remove paper backing from tab. Fuse tab in place.

3. Cut ½" notches along straight edge of jester ring. Insert cardboard circle into bottom of ring. Hot glue notched edge of ring to cardboard circle. Fuse fabric circle to bottom of container.

4. Stitch one jingle bell to each jester point with metallic thread.

5. Fill cellophane bag with fudge. Tie bag with ribbon. Place bag in jester hat. Add gift tag.

HOLIDAY HERB BUTTER

*T*his *creamy dill butter is great on crusty French bread, baked potatoes, grilled fish, or vegetables. Take some to your neighbor, along with a fresh loaf of bread tied up in holiday wrap and red raffia.*

GARLIC-DILL BUTTER

- ½ cup butter or margarine, softened
- ½ cup chopped fresh dill weed
- 1 tablespoon freshly squeezed lemon juice
- 1 clove garlic, minced

Process butter, dill weed, lemon juice, and garlic in a food processor until well blended. Store in an airtight container in refrigerator.

Yield: about ⅔ cup butter

BREAD AND BASKET WRAPPING

You will need two square Christmas napkins (we used 13" sq. napkins); loaf of French bread; red raffia; long, narrow bread basket; artificial greenery, pinecone, and berry sprig; glass jar with lid; Christmas spreader; and a gift card.

Fig. 1

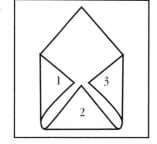

1. Spread one napkin flat and turn on point so it resembles a diamond. Fold

both side points and bottom point in toward center of napkin (Fig. 1). Fold edges 1 and 3 in to center again. Slip loaf of French bread into resulting pocket. Tie raffia into a bow around wrapped loaf of bread to hold wrapping secure.

2. Line bread basket with remaining napkin. Fill glass jar with Garlic-Dill Butter. Tie raffia into a bow around handle of glass jar lid. Place wrapped bread and jar of butter in lined basket. Tuck Christmas spreader in basket. Tuck greenery, pinecone, and berry sprig into side of basket. For tag, use marker to write recipe name or message on card. Tuck card in basket.

SANTA SUCKERS

Give the gift of whimsy this holiday season. Centered on lollipop sticks, these Santa sugar cookies make ideal favors for a children's party.

SANTA LOLLIPOP COOKIES

COOKIES
- ¾ cup butter or margarine, softened
- ½ cup confectioners sugar
- ½ cup granulated sugar
- 1 egg
- 1 teaspoon lemon extract
- 2½ cups all-purpose flour
- ¼ teaspoon salt
    4½-inch-long lollipop sticks

ICING
- 4½ cups sifted confectioners sugar
- 6 to 7 tablespoons half and half
- 1½ teaspoons lemon extract
    Blue and red paste food coloring

Preheat oven to 350 degrees. In a large bowl, cream butter and sugars until fluffy. Add egg and lemon extract; beat until smooth. In a small bowl, combine flour and salt. Add dry ingredients to creamed mixture; stir until a soft dough forms.

On a lightly floured surface, use a floured rolling pin to roll out half of dough to ¼-inch thickness. Use a 2¾ x 2¼-inch Santa-shaped cookie cutter or pattern, page 136, to cut out cookies. Transfer to a greased baking sheet, allowing space for sticks. Insert 2 inches of a stick into bottom of each cookie. Bake 8 to 10 minutes or until bottoms are lightly browned. Cool cookies on baking sheets 2 minutes; transfer to a wire rack to cool completely.

For icing, combine confectioners sugar, half and half, and lemon extract in a medium bowl; stir until smooth. Transfer 3 tablespoons icing to a small bowl; tint blue. Transfer ⅓ cup icing to another small bowl; tint red. Leave remaining icing white. Spoon each icing into a pastry bag fitted with a small round tip. Pipe white icing onto each cookie for hat trim and beard. Let icing harden slightly. Pipe red icing onto each cookie for hat, cheeks, and nose. Pipe blue icing onto each cookie for eyes. Let icing harden. Store in an airtight container.
Yield: about 2 dozen cookies

"HO HO HO" TAG

For each tag, you will need tracing paper, wrapping paper, white card stock, craft glue stick, black permanent fine-point marker, hole punch, and curling ribbon.

1. Trace tag pattern, page 136, onto tracing paper; cut out. Draw around pattern once on wrapping paper and twice on card stock; cut out.
2. Glue wrapping paper to one piece of card stock. Trim remaining piece of card stock ¼" on all sides; center and glue on top of wrapping paper-covered card stock.
3. Use marker to write message on tag. Punch hole in tag. Thread tag onto ribbon.

PEPPERMINT PARTY

A breeze to make, these cool peppermint mouthfuls will vanish before your eyes. Fill a candy jar with the chocolate-dipped treats and paint the lid to resemble pinwheel peppermint candy.

CRUSHED PEPPERMINT CREAMS

    1   jar (7 ounces) marshmallow
            creme
    ⅔   cup butter or margarine, softened
    1   teaspoon vanilla extract
    6   cups sifted confectioners sugar
    ¼   cup finely crushed peppermint
            candies (about 10 hard round
            candies)
    ½   cup (3 ounces) semisweet
            chocolate chips
    6   ounces chocolate candy coating

In a large bowl, beat marshmallow creme, butter, and vanilla extract until well blended. Gradually add confectioners sugar until mixture is well blended. Knead mixture by hand 2 to 3 minutes. Add crushed peppermint. Shape teaspoonfuls of candy into ¾-inch balls. Place on a baking sheet lined with waxed paper. Chill 1 hour or until firm.

Melt chocolate chips and candy coating in the top of a double boiler over hot water. Using a fork, dip candies halfway into melted chocolate, shaking off excess chocolate. Return to baking sheet lined with waxed paper. Chill until chocolate hardens. Store in an airtight container in a cool place.
Yield: about 7½ dozen candies

PEPPERMINT JARS

For each jar, you will need a glass jar with a 3¾"dia. round wooden lid, white spray paint, carbon paper, red acrylic paint, paintbrush, and clear acrylic spray sealer. (If using a glass jar with a lid larger than 3¾" dia., enlarge peppermint swirl pattern on a photocopier.)

Allow paint and sealer to dry after each application.

1. Remove rubber gasket from bottom of jar lid. Spray paint lid white.
2. Trace peppermint swirl pattern, page 137, onto scrap of paper. Use carbon paper and pencil to lightly transfer peppermint swirl pattern onto top of jar lid. Extend lines from top of lid onto sides of lid. Paint peppermint stripes red.
3. Spray lid with coat of clear acrylic sealer. Replace rubber gasket.

44

A SLEIGH FULL OF SWEETS

*S*hape and bake these chocolate cookie cups in minutes—two ingredients are all you need! Tuck a handful of the goodies in a cellophane bag and send them off to a friend in Santa's gold sleigh.

CHOCOLATE CHIP CRUNCH CUPS

1 package (18 ounces) refrigerated chocolate chip cookie dough
2 bars (1.55 ounces each) chocolate crispy rice candy bars, chopped (about ¾ cup candy)

Preheat oven to 350 degrees. Shape dough into 1-inch balls. Place balls into greased cups of a miniature muffin pan. Press down in center of each ball of dough to make a deep well. Spoon about 1 teaspoon chopped candy bar into center of each cup. Bake 10 to 12 minutes or until edges are firm. Cool in pan 5 minutes; remove to a wire rack to cool completely. Store in an airtight container. *Yield:* about 3 dozen cookies

SLEIGH PACKAGING

You will need a small cellophane bag; gold spray webbing; thin gold ribbon; hole punch (optional); gift tag; small, gold wire sleigh; gold glitter twigs; and a candy cane.

We found our gold wire sleigh in a dollar store. Gold glitter twigs can be found with dried florals in most crafts stores.

1. Lightly spray outside of cellophane bag with gold webbing; allow to dry. Fill cellophane bag with Chocolate Chip Crunch Cups. Tie gold ribbon into a bow around top of bag. Punch hole in gift tag if necessary and thread tag onto ribbon.
2. Place filled bag in wire sleigh. Tuck gold glitter twigs and candy cane in back of sleigh.

45

DOUBLE CHERRY DELIGHT

*C*herry pie fans will think they're in heaven when they taste this double cherry dessert sauce. With a kiss of almond flavor and some pineapple, too, the sauce is divine on ice cream, pound cake, or waffles. The recipe yields several jars, so you can spread some Christmas cheer with glasses and jars painted to celebrate the season.

CHERRY-ALMOND SAUCE

1   can (21 ounces) cherry pie filling
1   jar (10 ounces) maraschino
        cherries, drained
1   can (15¼ ounces) pineapple
        tidbits in juice
¼   cup firmly packed brown sugar
1½ teaspoons almond extract

In a medium saucepan, combine pie filling, cherries, tidbits with juice, and brown sugar. Stirring frequently, cook over medium heat until sugar dissolves. Remove from heat. Stir in almond extract; cool. Store in an airtight container in refrigerator.
Yield: about 4½ cups

DESSERT GLASSES AND MATCHING JARS

You will need small clear glass jars; clear dessert glasses; carbon paper; peel-and-stick vinyl shelf covering; craft knife; green, gold, and red glass paint; paintbrushes; hole punch (optional); gift tag; and ⅛"w satin ribbon.

Allow paint to dry after each application.

1. Refer to paint manufacturer's instructions to prepare glass surfaces for painting if necessary. Transfer holly pattern, page 132, onto scrap of paper. Using carbon paper, transfer pattern onto right side of vinyl shelf covering. Using craft knife, carefully cut out pattern. (You may prefer to use handle of paintbrush dipped into red paint to dot on holly berries instead of cutting.)
2. Center and adhere pattern stencil to side of a glass jar. Use green paint to paint holly leaves, gold paint to paint swirls, and red paint to paint holly berries. Reposition stencil and continue painting around side of jar until motifs meet. In same manner, paint holly motifs around rims of dessert glasses. Refer to paint manufacturer's instructions for how to cure paint and how to wash glasses.
3. Punch hole in gift tag if necessary. Write message on gift tag. Thread length of ribbon through hole in gift tag. Tie ribbon and gift tag around lid of glass jar. Package jar of sauce and several dessert glasses together and give as a set.

A coffee lover will sing your praises when you share our Coffee-and-Cream Brownies. The mocha-flavored sweets are a breeze to prepare when you start with a packaged brownie mix, and the handsome box holds other goodies later.

COFFEE-AND-CREAM BROWNIES

For extra coffee flavor, substitute brewed coffee for water in brownie mix.

- 1 package (about 23 ounces) brownie mix and ingredients to prepare brownies
- 2 tablespoons instant coffee granules
- 1 package (8 ounces) cream cheese, softened
- ½ cup confectioners sugar
- 1 egg
- ½ teaspoon vanilla extract

Preheat oven to 350 degrees. Line a 9 x 13-inch baking pan with aluminum foil, extending foil over ends of pan; grease foil. In a large bowl, prepare brownie mix according to package directions, stirring in coffee granules. Pour into prepared pan. In a medium bowl, beat cream cheese until fluffy. Beat in confectioners sugar, egg, and vanilla until well blended. Spoon dollops of cream cheese mixture over brownie batter. Swirl gently with tip of a knife.

Bake 33 to 38 minutes or until brownies begin to pull away from sides of pan and cream cheese swirls are lightly browned. Cool in pan on a wire rack. Use ends of foil to lift brownies

from pan. Cut into 2-inch squares. Store in an airtight container.
Yield: about 2 dozen brownies

COFFEE LOVER'S BOX

You will need a craft knife, cutting mat, 7" x 9" x 2½" papier-mâché box with a 9" x 11" top and bottom, ecru spray paint, plastic spoon, fabric, spray adhesive, 40" of ⅝"w brown grosgrain ribbon, photocopy of tag design (page 150) on ecru card stock, brown permanent fine-point marker, and a hot glue gun.

1. To cut slits for ribbon, use craft knife to cut one 1"w slit on each long side through top and bottom, close to sides of box. Spray paint box and spoon ecru; allow to dry.
2. Tear a 7" x 9" piece from fabric; fray edges. Apply spray adhesive to wrong side of fabric; center and smooth on top of box. Fill box with gift. Thread ribbon through slits and tie into a bow on top of box.
3. Cut out tag. Use marker to outline tag and draw over words. Hot glue tag to spoon. Place spoon handle under bow; hot glue to secure.

POT O' COOKIES

*C*hock-full of raisins, oats, and pecans, these hearty cookies really hit the spot! Create a folksy container for the treats by decorating a terra-cotta pot with fabric hearts and trim.

OATMEAL-RAISIN GRAHAM COOKIES

1   cup butter or margarine, softened
1   cup firmly packed brown sugar
½   cup granulated sugar
2   eggs
1   teaspoon vanilla extract
2   cups all-purpose flour
1   teaspoon baking powder
1   teaspoon baking soda
½   teaspoon salt
2   cups finely chopped cinnamon
      graham crackers, divided
1½ cups raisins
1   cup quick-cooking oats
1   cup chopped pecans, toasted

Preheat oven to 350 degrees. In a large bowl, cream butter and sugars until fluffy. Add eggs and vanilla; beat until smooth.

In a small bowl, combine flour, baking powder, baking soda, and salt. Add dry ingredients to creamed mixture; stir until a soft dough forms. Stir in 1 cup chopped crackers, raisins, oats, and pecans. Drop tablespoonfuls of dough into remaining chopped crackers, coating dough with crackers. Place 2 inches apart on a lightly greased baking sheet. Bake 8 to 10 minutes or until tops are lightly browned. Transfer cookies to a wire rack to cool. Store in an airtight container.
Yield: about 5 dozen cookies

APPLIQUÉD FLOWERPOT

You will need a 6" dia. terra-cotta flowerpot with saucer, assorted fabrics, craft glue, tracing paper, muslin, black permanent fine-point marker, resealable plastic bag, raffia, decorative-edge craft scissors, and ivory card stock.

Allow glue to dry after each application.

1. Measure around rim of flowerpot; add ½". Measure height of rim. Cut a strip from fabric the determined measurements. Overlapping at back, glue strip around rim.
2. Trace patterns, page 140, onto tracing paper; cut out. Follow *Making Appliqués,* page 153, to make one small heart and four large hearts from fabrics and four backgrounds from muslin.
3. Glue one large heart to each background. Arrange and glue backgrounds on front of flowerpot. Use marker to draw "stitches" around backgrounds.
4. Place cookies in plastic bag; place bag in flowerpot. Invert saucer and place on top of flowerpot for lid. Tie lengths of raffia into a bow around flowerpot and saucer.
5. For tag, use craft scissors to cut a 1¾" x 2½" piece from card stock. Glue small heart to tag. Use marker to draw "stitches" along edges and write message.

TAKE THE CAKE

*O*ur gooey glazed banana cake will stir up some compliments at your next dinner party.

GLAZED CHIFFON CAKE

CAKE
  2 cups all-purpose flour
1½ cups sugar
  1 tablespoon baking powder
  1 teaspoon salt
  6 eggs, separated
  1 cup mashed banana (about 2
      bananas)
 ½ cup vegetable oil
 ⅓ cup orange juice
  1 teaspoon grated orange zest
 ½ teaspoon cream of tartar

GLAZE
1½ cups sifted confectioners sugar
  2 tablespoons light corn syrup
  2 tablespoons orange juice
 ½ teaspoon grated orange zest

Preheat oven to 325 degrees. For cake, combine flour, sugar, baking powder, and salt. Make a well in center of dry ingredients and add egg yolks, banana, oil, orange juice, and orange zest; beat until smooth.

In a large bowl, beat egg whites and cream of tartar until stiff. Fold egg whites into batter. Pour in an ungreased 10-inch tube pan. Bake 1 hour 15 minutes or until a long toothpick inserted in center of cake comes out clean. Invert pan to cool. Remove cake from pan and place on plate.

For glaze, combine confectioners sugar, corn syrup, orange juice, and orange zest in a small bowl; stir until smooth. Spoon glaze over cake.
Yield: about 14 servings

CHIFFON CAKE BOX

You will need a 45" square of white chiffon, 10" sq. white cake box, 2 yds. of 1½"w white chiffon ribbon with gold edges, Christmas floral pick, openwork cake plate (optional), and 2 yds. of sheer ribbon (optional).

1. Lay chiffon square flat. Place cake in box. Place box diagonally in center of chiffon (Fig. 1).
2. Bring two diagonally opposite corners of fabric together; tie them into a knot. Bring remaining two corners of fabric together; tie them into a knot as well. Tuck ends of chiffon under.
3. Slip ribbon beneath fabric knots; tie into a multi-looped bow. Tuck floral pick beneath knots in ribbon.
4. If desired, rather than boxing up cake, place cake on plate with openwork design along rim. Thread sheer ribbon through holes as in photo. Tie ends of ribbon into a bow on top of plate.

Fig. 1

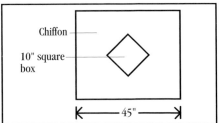

JOLLY JELLY BEAN MUFFINS

Merriment will abound Christmas morning when the kids catch sight of our jelly bean delights! Not your ordinary muffins, these goodies are made with orange juice and flavored jelly beans—a yummy surprise for young and old alike. Present the colorful cakes in an adorable reindeer basket.

JELLY BEAN MUFFINS

⅓ cup butter or margarine, softened
½ cup sugar
⅔ cup orange juice
1 egg
1½ cups all-purpose flour
2 teaspoons baking powder
½ teaspoon baking soda
½ teaspoon salt
½ cup small gourmet jelly beans, coarsely chopped

Preheat oven to 400 degrees. Line a muffin pan with foil muffin cups. In a large bowl, cream butter and sugar. Add orange juice and egg; beat until blended. In a small bowl, combine flour, baking powder, baking soda, and salt. Add dry ingredients to creamed mixture; stir just until moistened. Stir in jelly beans. Fill muffin cups about two-thirds full. Bake 13 to 15 minutes or until a toothpick inserted in center of muffin comes out clean. Remove from pan and cool on a wire rack. Store in an airtight container. *Yield:* about 1 dozen muffins

REINDEER BASKET

You will need tracing paper; white, red, and brown fuzzy felt; polyester fiberfill; package of dried lentils or small dried beans; black permanent fine-point marker; needle and thread; two (½") black buttons; hot glue gun; oval-shaped basket with bottom rim no larger than 5" x 8"; craft knife; two 9" long small tree twigs for antlers; 1⅓ yds. of 3½"w paper ribbon; and green shredded paper.

1. Trace patterns, pages 138 and 139, onto tracing paper; cut out. Using patterns, cut one tail from white felt; two noses from red felt; and one tail, two heads, two bodies, four ears, and eight feet from brown felt.
2. Using a ¼" seam allowance for all stitching, stitch tail pieces and ear pieces together to make one tail and two ears. Leaving a small opening for stuffing, stitch nose pieces together to make one nose and stitch feet pieces together to make four feet. Stuff nose and feet with fiberfill;

stitch openings closed. Pin feet and tail (white side down) to wrong side of one body piece. Pin ears to wrong side of one head piece. Leaving opening for stuffing, stitch pieces together to make one head and one body. Stuff head with fiberfill; stuff body with lentils. Stitch openings closed.
3. Use marker to draw paw marks on feet and line under nose. Using needle and thread, stitch button eyes in place on head.
4. Center and glue basket on body. Glue nose on head; glue head to top rim of basket. Use craft knife to cut slits in back of head for antlers. Insert ends of antlers through slits; glue to secure.
5. Tie paper ribbon around body and basket and into a bow behind head; notch ends of ribbon. Spot glue to secure.
6. Fill basket with paper shreds. Place gift in basket.

CRANBERRY ZING

*C*hristmas dinner comes to life when you add the zing of our Cranberry Butter to your table. This butter keeps well in the refrigerator so you can enjoy it throughout the holidays. The festive pail packs up an attractive gift.

CRANBERRY BUTTER

1   cup butter, softened
½   cup sweetened dried cranberries, finely chopped
1   teaspoon freshly grated orange zest

Combine butter, cranberries, and orange zest in a small bowl; stir until well-blended. Store in an airtight container in refrigerator.
Yield: about 1½ cups butter

DECORATED BUCKET

You will need an approximately 5¾"dia. galvanized bucket, artificial wired berries and leaves, hot glue gun (optional), cranberry-colored tissue paper, small clamp-top jar, 1½"w cranberry-colored wire-edged ribbon, and a gift card (optional).

1. Wrap handle of bucket with wired berries and leaves. If necessary, glue wired berries in place. Line bucket with tissue paper.
2. Fill jar with gift; replace lid on jar. Tie ribbon into a bow around rim of jar. Place jar in tissue-lined bucket. If desired, add gift card with recipe name written on card.

CANDIED CHRISTMAS

*P*op! Pop! Pop your way into the Christmas spirit! This hearty candy mix makes a great gift for families with children. The wide-mouth jar is just the right size for hungry little munchkins to scoop out a handful or two of mix.

CANDIED POPCORN AND PEANUTS

    10   cups freshly popped popcorn
     1   cup cocktail peanuts
    ½   cup butter or margarine
     1   cup firmly packed light brown sugar
    ¼   cup dark corn syrup
    ¼   teaspoon baking soda
    ¼   teaspoon salt
    ¼   teaspoon vanilla extract
     1   cup raisins

Combine popcorn and peanuts in a lightly greased roasting pan; stir well and set aside. Melt butter in a large saucepan; stir in sugar and corn syrup. Bring to a rolling boil. Boil 5 minutes, stirring occasionally. Remove mixture from heat; stir in soda, salt, and vanilla. Pour sugar mixture over popcorn mixture, stirring quickly with wooden spoon until evenly coated. Bake at 250 degrees for 45 minutes, stirring every 15 minutes. Stir in raisins; bake 15 additional minutes. Allow to cool and store in an airtight container. *Yield:* about 2¼ quarts candy

PAINTED JAR

You will need a large glass jar with screw-top lid; pre-cut tree and star sponges or pop-up craft sponges; green, yellow, and red glass paint; "HO" rubber stamp; spray

adhesive; approximately 7½" square of fabric; and jute twine.

Allow paint to dry after each application.

1. Referring to paint manufacturer's instructions, prepare glass surface to be painted if necessary. Soak pre-cut sponges in water; squeeze out excess water. If making your own sponge shapes, transfer tree and star patterns, page 134, onto pop-up sponge; cut out. Soak sponges in water; squeeze out excess water.
2. Using green glass paint and tree sponge and referring to *Sponge Painting*, page 154, sponge paint trees on sides of jar as desired. Using yellow glass paint and star sponge, paint a star on top of each tree. Using red glass paint and "HO" rubber stamp, stamp "HO, HO, HO" on sides of jar as desired.
3. Remove lid from jar. Lightly spray top of lid with spray adhesive. Center fabric square on top of lid and press into spray adhesive. Fill jar with gift and replace lid. Wrap jute twine around rim of lid several times and tie into a bow.
4. Refer to paint manufacturer's instructions for how to wash jar.

NAUGHTY OR NICE?

*O*ur *Lumps of Coal Cookies boast a rich, chocolaty flavor that's a holiday hit with kids—and grown-ups, too! Hide the merry morsels in a whimsical stocking made from kraft paper.*

LUMPS OF COAL COOKIES

1   package (22½ ounces) brownie
      mix and ingredients to prepare
      brownies
1½ cups quick-cooking oats
1   cup chopped pecans, toasted
1   cup white baking chips

Preheat oven to 350 degrees. In a large bowl, prepare brownies according to package directions, stirring in oats, pecans, and baking chips. Drop tablespoonfuls of dough 2 inches apart onto an ungreased baking sheet. Bake 9 to 11 minutes or until tops are set. Transfer cookies to a wire rack to cool. Store in an airtight container.
Yield: about 3½ dozen cookies

PAPER STOCKING

You will need paper-backed fusible web, fabric, tracing paper, kraft paper, coordinating sewing thread, ½"w paper-backed fusible web tape, 8" of ⅝"w grosgrain ribbon, hot glue gun, and a black permanent fine-point marker.

1. Using patterns, pages 140 and 141, and following *Making Appliqués,* page 153, make one heel and one toe appliqué from fabric. Make one 1½" x 6" cuff appliqué from fabric. Trace stocking pattern onto tracing paper; cut out. Draw around

pattern twice on kraft paper; cut out.
2. Arrange and fuse appliqués on one stocking piece. Zigzag stitch inside edges of cuff, heel, and toe. Place stocking pieces together; zigzag stitch outer edges of cuff, sides, heel, bottom of stocking, and toe together ⅛" from edges.
3. For hanger, cut one 1½" x 6" strip from fabric. Matching long edges and wrong sides, press strip in half. Unfold strip. Matching wrong sides, press each

long edge to pressed center mark. Following manufacturer's instructions, apply web tape along one folded edge of ribbon. Remove paper backing. Refold strip along center crease; press to secure. Matching short edges, fold hanger in half. Arrange ends of hanger at top of stocking; stitch to secure.
4. Tie ribbon into a bow. Glue bow to stocking. Use marker to write message on stocking. Fill stocking with gift.

STAND UP FOR APPLE PIE

*A*pples, raisins, and walnuts bake into a splendid pie to highlight any
Christmas celebration. The elegant pie stand is a gift that the recipient
will enjoy for years to come.

APPLE-RAISIN PIE

CRUST
- 2 cups all-purpose flour
- 1 teaspoon salt
- ¾ cup vegetable shortening
- 6 to 8 tablespoons cold water

FILLING
- 7 cups peeled, cored, and coarsely chopped baking apples (about 2½ pounds)
- 1 tablespoon freshly squeezed lemon juice
- ½ cup raisins
- ½ cup chopped toasted walnuts
- 1 teaspoon grated lemon zest
- ¾ cup firmly packed brown sugar
- 1 tablespoon cornstarch
- 1 teaspoon ground cinnamon
- ⅛ teaspoon salt
- 2 tablespoons butter, cut into small pieces
- 1 tablespoon milk
- 2 tablespoons granulated sugar

For crust, combine flour and salt in a medium bowl. Using a pastry blender or 2 knives, cut in shortening until mixture resembles coarse meal. Sprinkle with water; mix until a soft dough forms. Divide dough in half. On a lightly floured surface, use a floured rolling pin to roll out one half of dough to ⅛-inch thickness. Transfer to a 9-inch deep-dish pie plate.

Preheat oven to 375 degrees. For filling, place apples in a large bowl. Sprinkle lemon juice over apples. Stir in raisins, walnuts, and lemon zest. In a small bowl, combine brown sugar, cornstarch, cinnamon, and salt. Add dry ingredients to apple mixture; toss until well-coated. Spoon apple mixture into bottom crust. Place butter pieces over apple mixture. Roll out remaining half of dough to a 12-inch-diameter circle. Place crust over filling; use sharp knife to trim both edges of dough; seal and crimp edges. Brush crust with milk; sprinkle sugar over crust. Cut slits around center of pie. Bake 50 to 60 minutes or until fruit is tender and crust is golden brown. If crust browns too quickly, cover with a strip of aluminum foil. Cool pie on a wire rack.

Yield: about 8 to 10 servings

PIE STAND AND SERVER

You will need a gold pie stand with handle; variety of artificial greenery; florist wire; variety of artificial florals such as amaranthus, crab apple stem, pyracantha berry, birch cones, and dried apple slices; wooden pie server; hot glue gun; ribbon shredder; 1¼"w green-burgundy-and-gold plaid paper ribbon; and thin gold ribbon.

1. For pie stand, arrange artificial greenery as desired around handle; wire in place. Arrange florals (except apple slices) as desired; wire on top of artificial greenery.
2. For pie server, arrange greenery and then florals (except apple slices) as desired; wire entire arrangement together. Glue arrangement to base of handle of pie server.
3. For pie stand and pie server, shred lengths of plaid ribbon. Add thin shredded ribbon lengths and thin gold ribbon as accents on top of dried florals. Glue in place.
4. Glue one apple slice each to center of arrangement on pie stand and pie server. Cut length of plaid ribbon; tie into a bow. Glue bow behind apple slice on pie stand.

LIGHT UP A PARTY!

*S*park up your holiday party with this fruity punch. Place the chilled bottled punch in a bright light-bulb bag tied with colorful ribbons. Party guests are sure to request the recipe.

DELIGHTFUL PUNCH

- 3 bananas, cut into pieces
- 1 can (12 ounces) frozen pineapple juice concentrate
- 1 can (6 ounces) frozen lemonade concentrate
- 1 can (6 ounces) frozen orange juice concentrate
- 1 bottle (46 ounces) white grape juice
- 2 cups water
- 1 cup rum (optional)

Combine bananas and juice concentrates in batches in a blender or food processor; blend until smooth. Transfer mixture to a 1-gallon container. Stir in grape juice and water; add rum, if desired. Cover and store in refrigerator. Serve chilled.
Yield: about 12 cups punch

LIGHT-BULB BAG

You will need a 20" x 23" piece of light bulb-motif fabric, rubber band, 30" of 1"w sheer wired ribbon, several 30" lengths of assorted colors of ¼"w and ⅜"w satin ribbons, photocopy of tag design (page 150) on coordinating card stock, and a hole punch.

1. Matching right sides and long edges, follow *Making a Fabric Bag,* page 154, to make a bag from fabric.
2. Place gift in bag. Gather bag over gift; secure with rubber band. Tie ribbons together into a bow around top of bag, covering rubber band.
3. Cut out tag. Punch hole in top of tag. Thread tag onto one streamer from bow on bag.

MINTY CHOCOLATE CAKE

*M*ake light work of holiday baking with our Minty Chocolate Cake. Canned frosting makes icing the cake a breeze. Use the easy-to-embellish cake plate year-round to jazz up any dessert.

MINTY CHOCOLATE CAKE

- 1 package (18¼ ounces) devil's food cake mix
- 3 eggs
- 1½ cups water
- ⅓ cup vegetable oil
- 2 packages (4.67 ounces each) individually wrapped layered chocolate mints, divided
- 1 can (16 ounces) chocolate frosting

Preheat oven to 350 degrees. Grease two 9-inch round cake pans. Line bottoms with waxed paper; grease waxed paper. In a large bowl, combine cake mix, eggs, water, and oil. Mix according to package directions. Pour batter into prepared pans. Reserve 5 mints for garnish; set aside. Chop half the remaining mints and sprinkle over batter in pans, pressing slightly. Bake 25 to 30 minutes or until a toothpick inserted in center of cake comes out clean. Cool in pans 10 minutes. Turn out on a wire rack.

In a small saucepan, over medium-low heat, melt remaining half of mints. Spread over warm cake layers. Cool completely. Spread about ½ cup frosting over mint layer of one cake layer. Stack second layer on top; frost top and sides with remaining frosting. Use a vegetable peeler to shave curls from sides of 5 reserved mints; place on top of cake. Store in an airtight container.
Yield: about 12 servings

BAUBLE CAKE PLATE

You will need 12 clear glass baubles, 12 mint green glass baubles, E-6000 glue, and an approximately 13½" dia. clear glass cake plate.

Alternating colors and spacing baubles evenly, glue glass baubles around rim of plate, approximately ½" from outer rim of plate. Allow to dry. Wash cake plate by hand.

57

MAKE TIME FOR PIE!

*H*ere's a clever way to share oven-fresh convenience with friends on the go! Just pack easy-to-prepare Pie Crust Mix and dried fruit in no-sew fabric bags and deliver them in a pretty pie plate. Include the directions for mixing and baking an Apricot-Cranberry Pie, and your friends can enjoy a piping-hot treat whenever they want!

PIE CRUST MIX

You'll have enough mix to make several pie crusts.

- 8 cups all-purpose flour
- 2 tablespoons sugar
- 1½ tablespoons salt
- 2½ cups vegetable shortening

Combine flour, sugar, and salt in a large bowl. Using a pastry blender or 2 knives, cut in shortening until mixture resembles coarse meal. Store in an airtight container in refrigerator. Give with instructions for preparing crust.
Yield: about 11 cups mix

To prepare one 9-inch crust: Store mix in refrigerator until ready to prepare. Place 1½ cups mix in a medium bowl. Sprinkle with 3 to 4 tablespoons cold water; mix until a soft dough forms. On a lightly floured surface, use a floured rolling pin to roll out dough to ⅛-inch thickness. Transfer to a 9-inch pie plate and use a sharp knife to trim edge of dough. If crust has a filling, bake according to recipe. If crust is baked before adding filling, bake in a 450-degree oven 10 to 12 minutes or until golden brown. Let cool before adding filling.

To prepare one 9-inch double crust: Prepare using 2 cups mix and 5 to 7 tablespoons cold water. Divide dough in half and roll out each half following instructions for single crust. Bake according to recipe.

APRICOT-CRANBERRY PIE

- 2 cups water
- 1 package (6 ounces) sweetened dried cranberries
- 1 package (6 ounces) dried apricots, coarsely chopped
- 1 cup sugar
- 3 tablespoons cornstarch
- ½ teaspoon salt
- 2 tablespoons apricot brandy
- 2 cups Pie Crust Mix
- 1 tablespoon butter
  Sugar

Preheat oven to 375 degrees. In a medium saucepan, bring water, cranberries, and apricots to a boil over medium heat. Remove from heat. Cover and let stand 10 minutes.

In a small bowl, combine 1 cup sugar, cornstarch, and salt. Return fruit mixture to medium heat. Gradually stir in dry ingredients; cook over medium heat until thickened. Remove from heat; stir in brandy.

Place 2 cups pie crust mix in a medium bowl; sprinkle 5 to 7 tablespoons cold water over mix, stirring until a soft dough forms. Divide dough in half. On a lightly floured surface, use a floured rolling pin to roll out half of dough to ⅛-inch thickness. Transfer to a 9-inch pie plate and use a sharp knife to trim edges of dough. Roll out remaining dough to ⅛-inch thickness. Use a 1-inch-wide heart-shaped cookie cutter to cut out hearts in top crust. Spoon filling into prepared crust. Dot with butter. Place top crust over filling. Flute edges of dough and sprinkle top with sugar. Bake 35 to 40 minutes or until crust is golden brown and filling is bubbly. Serve warm.
Yield: about 8 servings

HOMESPUN BAGS

For each bag, you will need ½"w paper-backed fusible web tape, one 4" square and one 7½" x 20" piece of fabric, paper-backed fusible web, kraft paper, craft glue, 1½" x 2½" piece of ecru card stock, black permanent fine-point marker, and 27" of jute twine.

1. Fuse web tape along each long edge on right side of 7½" x 20" piece of fabric; do not remove paper backing. Matching right sides and short edges, press fabric in half (fold is bottom of bag). Unfold fabric. Remove paper backing. Refold fabric; fuse edges together.
2. Fuse tape along top edge of bag on wrong side of fabric; do not remove paper backing. Press edge 1" to wrong side, unfold, and remove paper backing; fuse edge in place. Turn bag right side out.
3. Refer to *Making Appliqués,* page 153, to make one 2½" x 3½" appliqué from 4" square of fabric (do not remove paper backing) and one 2" x 3" appliqué from kraft paper square. Using marker, draw border and write message on kraft paper label. Fuse kraft paper to fabric. Remove paper-backing from fabric square; fuse fabric square to bag. Glue card stock to kraft paper; allow to dry. Place gift in bag. Tie twine into a bow around top of bag.

59

KRIS KRINGLE CHOCOLATES

With these giant chocolates around, Kris Kringle might just slide down the chimney early. Peanuts, rice cereal, and chocolate make a candy that puts everyone into the holiday spirit. Wrapped in colorful cellophane, these are perfect for a chocolate lover.

GIANT KRIS KRINGLE CHOCOLATES

  1 (12-ounce) package semisweet chocolate chips
 ½ cup butter or margarine
 ½ cup light corn syrup
  1 cup sifted powdered sugar
  2 teaspoons vanilla extract
  3 cups toasted rice cereal
  1 cup cocktail peanuts
  1 cup raisins

Combine chocolate chips, butter, and corn syrup in a 2-quart heavy saucepan; cook until chocolate melts. Remove from heat; stir in sugar and vanilla. Combine cereal, peanuts, and raisins in a large bowl. Pour chocolate mixture over cereal mixture; toss until thoroughly coated. Cool to room temperature. Divide mixture into 5 equal portions (about 1 cup each). Butter a 4-inch-diameter funnel; with buttered hands, pack mixture, one portion at a time, into funnel. Unmold onto waxed paper-lined baking sheet. Wipe funnel with paper towel and butter again before repeating packing procedure with remaining mixture. Refrigerate 2 hours or until hardened. Cover and store in refrigerator.
Yield: 5 giant chocolates

CHOCOLATE DROP PACKAGING

You will need red, green, or silver Mylar™ or clear cellophane and a variety of ribbons or curling ribbon.

1. Cut an approximately 16" to 18" square of Mylar or cellophane. Place gift in center of square and, referring to photo, gather at top of chocolate.

2. Tie ribbon or curling ribbon into a bow at top of gift.

*T*his spicy mix warms up cold weather blues—the recipe makes enough for several gifts. A pretty poinsettia basket brightens a kitchen counter throughout the season.

ITALIAN SNACK MIX

- ½ cup butter or margarine, melted
- 1 tablespoon white wine vinegar
- 1 package (0.7 ounce) Italian salad dressing mix
- ¼ teaspoon salt
- 8 cups bite-size crispy corn-rice cereal
- 1 package (10 ounces) small pretzel twists
- 1 can (11½ ounces) mixed nuts
- ¼ cup grated Romano or Parmesan cheese

Preheat oven to 250 degrees. In a small bowl, combine butter, vinegar, dressing mix, and salt. In a large roasting pan, combine cereal, pretzels, and nuts. Pour butter mixture over cereal mixture; stir until well coated.

Bake 1 hour, stirring every 15 minutes. Sprinkle with cheese and stir. Spread on aluminum foil to cool. Store in an airtight container.

Yield: about 17 cups snack mix

POINSETTIA CRATE BASKET

You will need poinsettia-motif fabric, paper-backed fusible web, any type of basket (we used a 5½" sq. wooden basket with grapevine handle), 5" x 10" clear plastic bag, and 20" of 1½"w wired ribbon.

1. Use one poinsettia motif from fabric and follow *Making Appliqués*, page 153, to make one poinsettia appliqué. Remove paper backing. Fuse appliqué to basket.

2. Place gift in bag. Tie ribbon into a bow around top of bag. Place bag in basket.

BASKET FULL OF PEPPERS

*D*illed red and green pepper chunks add festive color to your holiday plate. Remember to make at least five days ahead to ensure the best flavor. Serve them chilled and get rave reviews. Package in a seasonal basket and give in time for Christmas dinner.

DILL PEPPER CHUNKS

- 3 sweet red peppers, cut into 1-inch pieces (about 4½ cups)
- 3 green peppers, cut into 1-inch pieces (about 4½ cups)
- 5 sprigs fresh dill weed
- 5 cloves garlic
- 3 cups white vinegar
- 3 cups water
- ¾ cup sugar
- 3 tablespoons canning and pickling salt

Pack pepper pieces into 5 heat-resistant pint jars with lids, adding a sprig of dill weed and garlic clove to each jar. In a medium saucepan, combine vinegar, water, sugar, and salt. Stirring occasionally, bring mixture to a boil over medium-high heat. Pour hot liquid over pepper pieces; cover and cool to room temperature. Store in refrigerator 5 days to let flavors develop. Serve chilled.
Yield: 5 pints peppers

GIFT CARD AND JAR LID COVER

You will need a pint jar with lid, fabric, rubber band, ⅜"w ribbon, envelope, red and white card stock, green corrugated craft cardboard, craft glue stick, decorative-edge craft scissors, red handmade paper, Christmas sticker, Christmas greeting motif from wrapping paper, black permanent fine-point marker, yellow permanent fine-point marker, green shredded paper, and a basket (we used a 6" x 8½" basket).

1. Remove lid from jar. Draw around jar lid on wrong side of fabric; cut out circle 2½" outside drawn line. Place gift in jar; replace lid on jar. Center circle over lid; secure with rubber band.
2. Measure around jar lid; add 15". Cut a length from ribbon the determined measurement. Tie ribbon into a bow around jar lid, covering rubber band.
3. Measure height of front of envelope. Cut a ⅝"w strip from red card stock and a ½"w strip from cardboard the determined measurement. Glue card stock strip to envelope; then glue cardboard strip to card stock strip.
4. For card, measure height and width of front of envelope; subtract ¼" from each measurement. Cut a piece from red card stock the determined measurements. Fold card stock in half, matching short edges.
5. Measure height and width of front of card; subtract ¼" from each measurement. Use decorative-edge scissors to cut a piece from cardboard the determined measurements. Measure height and width of cardboard; subtract ½" from each measurement. Use decorative-edge scissors to cut a piece from white card stock the determined measurements. Tear a 2½" x 3½" piece from handmade paper. Center and glue handmade paper to card stock; then glue card stock to cardboard. Glue cardboard to front of card. Apply sticker to handmade paper. Glue greeting motif inside card.
6. Use black marker to write message along edges of card stock. If desired, use yellow marker to color stars.
7. Fill basket with shredded paper. Place gift in basket; tuck in gift card.

TEA CAKE BREAK

Packaged in a jar embellished with festive ribbon and tiny ornaments, Orange Tea Cakes are a welcome gift for the holiday weary.

ORANGE TEA CAKES

- ¾ cup butter or margarine, softened
- ½ cup confectioners sugar, sifted
- ½ cup granulated sugar
- 1 egg
- 1 teaspoon orange extract
- 2½ cups all-purpose flour
- ¼ teaspoon salt

Preheat oven to 350 degrees. In a large bowl, cream butter and sugars until fluffy. Add egg and orange extract; beat until smooth. In a small bowl, combine flour and salt. Add dry ingredients to creamed mixture; stir until a soft dough forms. Divide dough in half. Wrap one half in plastic wrap. On a lightly floured surface, use a floured rolling pin to roll out other half of dough to ⅛-inch thickness. Use a 3-inch round scalloped-edge cookie cutter to cut out cookies. Transfer to a greased baking sheet. Bake 7 to 9 minutes or until bottoms are lightly browned. Transfer cookies to a wire rack to cool. Repeat with remaining dough. Store in an airtight container.

Yield: about 4½ dozen cookies

COOKIE JAR

You will need a square, flat-topped, clear glass cookie jar; thick tacky glue; miniature Christmas balls, packages, candy canes, or other Christmas ornaments; 1½"w ribbon; and a hot glue gun (optional).

Allow tacky glue to dry after each application.

1. Remove lid from jar. Using tacky glue, glue miniature ornaments to top of lid as desired.

2. Tie ribbon into a bow around jar. If necessary, hot glue ribbon in place. Using hot glue or tacky glue, glue several miniature ornaments to center of bow. Fill jar with gift; replace lid.

PLUM OF A HOLIDAY!

*A*dding *Plum Honey to the Christmas morning menu will entice everyone away from Santa's delivery long enough for breakfast. Canned plums make this gift a cinch to stir together.*

PLUM HONEY

3   cans (15¼ ounces each) whole
      purple plums, drained, pitted,
      and chopped
1   jar (12 ounces) orange
      marmalade
2   cups honey

Place plums and marmalade in a large microwave-safe bowl. Microwave on high power (100%) 2 minutes or until marmalade melts. Stir in honey until well blended. Store in an airtight container in refrigerator. Serve with breads or use as a glaze for meat.

Yield: about 5½ cups honey

JAR AND HONEY DIPPER

You will need a jar with a rubber-stopper lid; 1¼"w plum-colored, sheer, wire-edged ribbon; hot glue gun; artificial holly and holly berry sprigs; and a wooden honey dipper.

1. Remove lid from jar. Following *Making a Bow,* page 153, tie wire-edged ribbon into a multi-looped bow around neck of jar. Glue holly leaves and berries to center of bow. Remove lid from jar. Fill jar with gift; replace lid.

2. For honey dipper, tie ribbon into a small bow around top of handle. Glue small sprig of holly and berries to center of bow.

CRUNCH FOR CHRISTMAS

*T*his rich peanut butter spread satisfies the child in all of us. And candy canes give a new spin to holiday packaging. Slather this yummy snack on graham crackers and take a break from wrapping presents.

CROCK FULL OF CRUNCH

    1   (16-ounce) jar peanut butter
    ½   cup almond brickle chips
    ½   cup semisweet chocolate mini
            chips

Combine all ingredients, stirring well. Spoon into a gift container; cover and store in refrigerator. To serve, spread on graham crackers, vanilla wafers, or bananas.
Yield: 2½ cups spread

CANDY CANE JAR

You will need an 8" round jar with pop-in lid, two heavy-duty rubber bands, 40 (6"-tall) candy canes in clear cellophane wrappers, thick tacky glue, 1¼ yds. of 1½"w red-and-green ribbon, and two Christmas charms or shank buttons (remove shanks with wire cutters).

Allow tacky glue to dry after each application.

1. Remove lid from jar. Place rubber bands around jar 1" from top and bottom edges. Referring to photo, position candy canes (still in wrappers) between rubber bands and jar, encircling jar.
2. Pull a few candy canes away from top edge of jar; squeeze tacky glue behind them. Reposition candy canes. Repeat for

remaining candy canes. Make sure all candy canes are standing up straight.
3. Move rubber bands to middle of candy canes. Tie ribbon into a bow around candy canes on top of rubber bands.

Trim ends of ribbon.
4. Glue one charm or button to knot of bow; glue one charm or button to top of jar lid.
5. Fill jar with gift; replace lid.

SOPHISTICATED POPS

*C*reated for adult palates, these spirited coffee-flavored treats take a simple pleasure of childhood and give it a sophisticated grown-up twist. A canister filled with After-Dinner Lollipops will sweeten a friend's day.

AFTER-DINNER LOLLIPOPS

Vegetable oil cooking spray
32 lollipop sticks
2 cups sugar
1 cup strongly brewed coffee
⅔ cup light corn syrup
⅓ cup coffee-flavored liqueur

Heavily spray a baking sheet with cooking spray. Place lollipop sticks about 3 inches apart on baking sheet. In a heavy saucepan, combine sugar, coffee, and corn syrup. Stirring constantly, cook over medium-low heat until sugar dissolves. Cover and cook 2 to 3 minutes to wash down any sugar crystals on sides of pan. Attach a candy thermometer to pan, making sure thermometer does not touch bottom of pan. Increase heat to medium and bring to a rolling boil. Cook, without stirring, until mixture reaches 292 degrees. Test about ½ teaspoon mixture in ice water. Mixture will form brittle threads in ice water and will remain brittle when removed from water. Remove from heat. Stir in liqueur. Spoon about 1 tablespoon hot candy over 1 end of each lollipop stick to form a 2½-inch-diameter circle. Let candy cool. Wrap individually in small plastic bags or plastic wrap. Store in an airtight container.
Yield: 32 lollipops

BOW-TIED CANISTER AND TAG

You will need a photocopy of tag design (page 151) on tan card stock, colored pencils, black permanent fine-point marker, hole punch, glass canister (we used a 4½" x 9" glass canister), 1½ yds. of 1½"w wired ribbon, and 8" of gold cord.

1. Cut out tag. Use colored pencils to color tag. Use marker to write message on tag. Punch a hole at top of tag.
2. Place gift in canister; replace lid. Tie ribbon into a bow around canister. Use cord to attach tag to bow.

STAR STRUCK

You'll be the star of the neighborhood when you deliver this double chocolate pie. Its flaky cocoa crust and chocolaty filling create a truly decadent dessert. For a memorable gift, place the pie in a starry box and tie with shiny gold ribbon.

CHOCOLATE-PECAN PIE

COCOA CRUST
- 1 cup all-purpose flour
- ¼ cup sugar
- 3 tablespoons cocoa
- ¼ teaspoon salt
- ½ cup chilled butter or margarine, cut into pieces
- 1 egg yolk
- ½ teaspoon vanilla extract
- 2 to 4 teaspoons water

FILLING
- 1 cup dark corn syrup
- ½ cup firmly packed brown sugar
- 6 ounces semisweet baking chocolate, chopped
- 3 tablespoons butter or margarine
- 3 eggs
- 1 teaspoon vanilla extract
- ⅛ teaspoon salt
- 1½ cups chopped pecans, toasted
  Whipped cream to serve

For cocoa crust, combine flour, sugar, cocoa, and salt in a medium bowl. Using a pastry blender or 2 knives, cut in butter until mixture resembles coarse meal. Add egg yolk, vanilla, and water; mix until a soft dough forms. Roll out dough to a 10-inch round between sheets of plastic wrap. Chill 20 minutes. Transfer to a 9-inch pie plate and use a sharp knife to trim edge of dough. Flute edge of dough. Cover with plastic wrap and chill 1 hour.

Preheat oven to 400 degrees. For filling, combine corn syrup and brown sugar in a medium saucepan. Stirring constantly, bring mixture to a simmer over medium-high heat (about 3 minutes). Remove from heat. Add chocolate and butter; stir until smooth. Transfer to a heat-resistant bowl and let cool 10 minutes. In a medium bowl, beat eggs, vanilla, and salt. Beat in chocolate mixture. Stir in pecans. Bake crust 5 minutes. Reduce heat to 350 degrees. Pour filling into crust. Bake 35 to 40 minutes or until filling is almost set. Cool on a wire rack. Serve with whipped cream.
Yield: about 8 servings

STAR-STAMPED PIE BOX

You will need pop-up craft sponges, 10½" x 2" white box, gold metallic acrylic paint, paper plate, glass plate, white tissue paper with gold stars, 1½"w gold metallic ribbon, and a hot glue gun.

If you cannot find white tissue with gold stars, make your own by stamping gold stars, as described below, onto plain white tissue paper.
Allow paint to dry after each application.

1. Using scrap of paper, make paper patterns of large and small stars, page 137. Trace around patterns on craft sponges; cut out. Soak sponges in water; squeeze out any excess water.
2. Separate box lid and bottom; place both on table so that outside of box is faceup. Pour puddle of paint onto paper plate. Referring to *Sponge Painting,* page 154, sponge paint outside of box lid and bottom as desired.
3. Place pie on glass plate. Line bottom of box with tissue paper. Place gift in box bottom. Fold tissue paper into box over pie. Cut length of ribbon and wrap across top of box lid and to inside; glue ends of ribbon to inside of box lid. Referring to photo and *Making a Bow,* page 153, tie a multi-looped bow; glue to top center of box. Place box lid on box bottom.

"THAI" UP CHRISTMAS

*P*eanut Sauce over pasta lends a touch of Thailand to a holiday meal. Give this gift with simple heating instructions and uncooked pasta. The napkin rings are a fun finishing touch to a table setting.

PEANUT SAUCE

1½	cups lightly salted roasted peanuts
1	onion, coarsely chopped
½	cup water
6	cloves garlic
1	jalapeño pepper, seeded
1½	teaspoons ground coriander
½	teaspoon ground cumin
½	teaspoon dried grated lemon peel
½	teaspoon ground ginger
¼	cup vegetable oil
5	tablespoons all-purpose flour
3	cups milk
¼	cup granulated sugar
¼	cup soy sauce
1	tablespoon lemon juice
1	pound tri-colored corkscrew pasta, cooked according to package instructions to serve

In a blender or food processor, process first 9 ingredients until mixture is a smooth paste.

In a large saucepan, heat oil over medium heat. Stir in flour; cook 1 minute. Stir in peanut mixture. Gradually stir in milk. Stirring constantly, cook until thickened. Stirring constantly, add sugar, soy sauce, and lemon juice; cook until heated through. Serve warm over pasta or cover and chill until ready to heat and serve.

Yield: about 8 servings

NAPKIN RINGS AND MATCHING CANISTERS

You will need green, yellow, and red Fun Foam; variety of colorful buttons; tacky glue; two square airtight glass canisters; stapler; dish towel; and a basket.

Allow tacky glue to dry after each application.

1. Use scrap of paper to make tree and star patterns, page 137. Trace tree pattern onto green Fun Foam and star pattern onto yellow Fun Foam as many times as desired. Cut out shapes. For each napkin ring, also cut one 1¼" x 7¼" strip from red Fun Foam.

2. Glue buttons to one side of each star and tree as desired. Glue stars and/or trees to sides of canisters as desired.

3. For napkin rings, fold each 1¼" x 7¼" strip into a circle, overlapping ends slightly; staple ends together. Center and glue one tree or one star on each red foam circle, positioning tree or star opposite stapled edges.

4. Fill canisters with gifts. Place filled canisters in a dish towel-lined basket.

LET IT SNOW!

*Y*ou don't need snow to make a snowman—snowman cookies, that is. Kids delight in these frosty fellows, complete with hat and scarf. Make sure the icing has hardened before placing cookies in a basket.

SNOWMAN COOKIES

COOKIES
- ¾ cup butter or margarine, softened
- ½ cup granulated sugar
- ½ cup confectioners sugar
- 1 egg
- 1½ teaspoons clear vanilla extract
- 2¼ cups all-purpose flour
- ½ teaspoon baking soda
- ½ teaspoon cream of tartar

ICING
- 4 cups confectioners sugar
- 6 tablespoons water
- 3 tablespoons meringue powder
- 1½ teaspoons clear vanilla extract
  Red, blue, and green paste food coloring

In a large bowl, cream butter and sugars until fluffy. Add egg and vanilla; beat until smooth. In a medium bowl, combine flour, baking soda, and cream of tartar. Add dry ingredients to creamed mixture; stir until a soft dough forms. Divide dough in half. Wrap in plastic wrap and chill 2 hours.

Preheat oven to 350 degrees. On a lightly floured surface, use a floured rolling pin to roll out half of dough to slightly less than ¼-inch thickness. Cut out cookies using a 2¾ x 1⅞-inch snowman-shaped cookie cutter. Transfer to a lightly greased baking sheet. Bake 7 to 9 minutes or until bottoms are lightly browned. Transfer cookies to a wire rack to cool.

For icing, beat confectioners sugar, water, meringue powder, and vanilla at high speed of an electric mixer in a medium bowl 7 to 10 minutes or until stiff. Transfer ½ cup icing each into 3 small bowls; tint icing red, blue, and green. Leave remaining icing white. Adding ¼ teaspoon water at a time, add enough water to tinted and white icing until each icing flows smoothly when dropped from a spoon. Spoon each colored icing into a pastry bag fitted with a small round tip. Spread white icing on each cookie for body of snowman. Allow icing to harden on each cookie slightly. Use desired tinted icing to pipe hat, scarf, eyes, nose, and mouth onto each cookie. Let icing harden. Store in an airtight container.

Yield: about 3½ dozen cookies

SCARF BASKETS

You will need red polar fleece, small grapevine baskets, and tissue paper.

1. Cut approximately 1"w strips of red polar fleece. Fringe approximately 1" of each short end. Referring to photo, wrap a polar fleece strip around each basket; tie into a knot.

2. Fill basket with tissue paper. Place cookies in baskets.

PEPPERMINT PERFECTION

*D*ivinity doesn't get any better than this. The soft peppermint gives the candy a flavor that is light and refreshing. Take this divinity as a hostess gift for a great after-dinner treat.

PEPPERMINT DIVINITY

    2   cups sugar
    ½   cup light corn syrup
    ½   cup water
    ⅛   teaspoon salt
    3   egg whites
    ½   cup finely crushed soft peppermint
          candy sticks (about
          2 ounces or 5½ sticks)
    1   teaspoon vanilla extract
          Additional finely crushed soft
          peppermint candy (optional)

Butter sides of a heavy saucepan. Combine sugar, corn syrup, water, and salt. Stirring constantly, cook over medium heat until sugar dissolves. Using a pastry brush dipped in hot water, wash down any sugar crystals on sides of hot pan. Attach a candy thermometer to pan, making sure thermometer does not touch bottom of pan. Increase heat to medium-high and bring to a boil. When syrup nears 250 degrees, beat egg whites in a large bowl until stiff using highest speed of an electric mixer. Cook, without stirring, until syrup reaches hard-ball stage (approximately 260 to 268 degrees). Test about ½ teaspoon syrup in ice water. Syrup will roll into a hard ball in ice water and will remain hard when removed from water. Remove syrup from heat. While beating with an electric mixer on medium speed, pour syrup over egg whites. Increase speed of mixer to high and continue to

beat just until mixture holds its shape, 3 to 4 minutes. Fold in peppermint candy and vanilla. Quickly drop by teaspoonfuls onto waxed paper. Immediately sprinkle with additional peppermint candy, if desired. Store in an airtight container.
Yield: 1½ pounds divinity

PAINTED TIN

You will need a plain white tin, red glass paint, small paintbrush, black permanent fine point marker, sponge paintbrush, clear acrylic sealer, and red tissue paper.

Allow paint and acrylic sealer to dry after each application.

1. Use scrap piece of paper to make pattern of ornament, page 141. Using pencil, trace around ornament on lid of tin as desired.
2. Referring to photo for inspiration and using red glass paint and small paintbrush, paint each ornament with swirls, stripes, polka dots, or as a solid ornament. (To make polka dots, dip handle of paintbrush into red paint and dot on paint.)
3. Using permanent marker, outline each ornament; draw a cap and hook at top.
4. Using sponge paintbrush, paint entire lid with coat of acrylic sealer; paint lid with second coat of acrylic sealer.
5. Line bottom of tin with red tissue. Fill tin with gift.

HOSPITALITY FRUIT DIP

*P*resented with a basket of fresh fruit, a jar of Piña Colada Fruit Dip makes a welcome gift for a new neighbor. Coconut-flavored rum enhances the tropical taste sensation. We chose a basket with a pineapple motif as a symbol of hospitality.

PIÑA COLADA FRUIT DIP

1 package (8 ounces) cream cheese, softened
¼ cup coconut-flavored rum
¼ cup cream of coconut
¼ cup frozen grated coconut, thawed
2 tablespoons pineapple gelatin
1 container (8 ounces) piña colada yogurt

In a medium bowl, beat cream cheese until fluffy. Beat in rum, cream of coconut, coconut, and dry gelatin. Fold in yogurt. Store in an airtight container in refrigerator. Serve with fresh fruit.
Yield: about 2¾ cups dip

PINEAPPLE BASKET AND TAG

You will need a basket (we used an 8" dia. wire basket with a wire pineapple shape on handle), wrapping paper, ecru card stock, spray adhesive, tracing paper, colored pencils, gold fine-point paint pen, black permanent fine-point marker, and fresh fruit.

1. Measure around widest part of basket; add 4". Measure inside height of basket; double number and add 6". Cut a piece from wrapping paper the determined measurements. Matching wrong sides and

long edges, fold wrapping paper in half. Placing fold along rim of basket, line inside of basket with wrapping paper. Fill basket with fresh fruit.

2. For tag, cut a 3" x 10½" piece each from card stock and wrapping paper. Apply spray adhesive to wrong side of wrapping paper; smooth onto card stock. Matching wrong sides and short edges,

fold tag in half.

3. Trace pineapple pattern, page 151, onto tracing paper; cut out. Draw around pattern on card stock; cut out ¼" outside drawn line. Use colored pencils to color pineapple. Use paint pen to outline pineapple. Use marker to write message on pineapple. Apply spray adhesive to wrong side of pineapple; smooth onto tag.

NO-SEW BAKING

*B*utton cookies cleverly combine a love of baking with a love of sewing.
*Just tie the cooled cookies together to create small stacks. Once all the
cookies are gone, the basket is just right for a sewing kit.*

BUTTON COOKIES

  ¾ cup butter or margarine, softened
  1 cup confectioners sugar
  1 egg
  1 teaspoon almond extract
2½ cups all-purpose flour
  ¼ teaspoon salt
  ⅛-inch-wide red and green satin
        ribbon to decorate, if desired

In a large bowl, cream butter and sugar until fluffy. Add egg and almond extract; beat until smooth. In a small bowl, combine flour and salt. Add dry ingredients to creamed mixture; stir until a soft dough forms. Divide dough in half. Wrap in plastic wrap and chill 1 hour or until firm.

Preheat oven to 350 degrees. On a lightly floured surface, use a floured rolling pin to roll out half of dough to ¼-inch thickness. Use a 2-inch round cookie cutter to cut out cookies. Transfer to a greased baking sheet. Using the top of a 1½-inch-diameter glass, press an indentation into each cookie. Using a drinking straw, punch four holes in center of each cookie to resemble holes for thread.

Bake 7 to 9 minutes or until bottoms are lightly browned. Transfer cookies to a wire rack to cool. Repeat with remaining dough. Store in an airtight container. If desired, cookies can be stacked and tied together with ribbon.
Yield: about 3½ dozen cookies

PADDED LID BASKET

You will need a round basket (we used an 8" dia. basket), drawing compass, corrugated cardboard, black permanent fine-point marker, polyester low-loft batting, fabric, hot glue gun, 1" dia. button, hammer, thin nail, craft wire, 1" dia. wooden ball, colored pencils, photocopy of tag design (page 150) on ecru card stock, hole punch, and one strand of raffia.

1. Measure diameter of basket. Use compass to draw two circles on cardboard the determined measurement. Cut out one circle along drawn line; cut out remaining circle 1" inside drawn line.

2. Using large circle as pattern, use marker to draw around circle on batting and on wrong side of fabric. Cut out batting circle along drawn line; cut out fabric circle 2" outside of drawn line. Center batting circle on large cardboard circle; center fabric circle on batting circle. Clipping as necessary, smooth and glue fabric circle to bottom side of large cardboard circle.

3. Draw around remaining cardboard circle on wrong side of fabric; cut out 2" outside drawn line. Center fabric circle on cardboard circle. Clipping as necessary, glue fabric circle to bottom of cardboard circle.

4. Place bottoms of circles together; glue lid to secure. Glue button to center of padded lid. Use hammer and nail to make two holes through button holes and through lid. Use wire to adhere button tightly through all layers to indent padding. Glue ball to button.

5. Use pencils to color tag. Use marker to write message on tag. Cut out tag. Punch a hole in tag. Use raffia to attach tag to ball on lid. Fill basket with gift.

to my favorite quilting pal

HAVE A BALL

Surprise your party hostess with the gift of a cheese ball. Honey adds a bit of sweetness to the sharp Cheddar, while toasted almonds lend contrast and texture to the soft cheeses. The fabric-covered basket makes it easy to grab and go.

HONEY-OF-A-CHEESE BALL

- 2 cups (8 ounces) shredded sharp Cheddar cheese
- 1 cup (4 ounces) shredded mild Cheddar cheese
- 1 package (3 ounces) cream cheese, softened
- 3 tablespoons honey
- 2 tablespoons Dijon-style mustard
- $\frac{2}{3}$ cup sliced almonds, toasted and chopped

Process Cheddar cheeses, cream cheese, honey, and mustard in a food processor until well blended. Shape into a ball and roll in chopped almonds. Wrap in plastic wrap and chill overnight to let flavors blend. Serve at room temperature with crackers.
Yield: about 2¼ cups cheese

FABRIC-COVERED BASKET

You will need a round basket (we used a 10" dia. basket), fabric, string, fabric marking pen, thumbtack, rubber band, 2½"w wired ribbon, hot glue gun, shredded paper, clear plastic bag, and a scrap of red ribbon.

1. Beginning at rim and measuring under basket to opposite rim, measure basket (Fig. 1); add 4". Cut a square from fabric the determined measurement.
2. Matching right sides, fold fabric square in half from top to bottom and again from left to right. Tie one end of string to fabric marking pen. Referring to Step 1, measure half the determined measurement from pen; insert thumbtack through string at this point. Insert thumbtack through fabric and, keeping string taut, mark cutting line (Fig. 2). Cutting through all layers, cut out circle along drawn line.
3. Unfold circle. Center basket on wrong side of circle. Fold edge of circle 2" to wrong side. Gather circle around basket under rim; secure with rubber band.
4. Wrap ribbon twice around basket to cover rubber band. Tie ends into a knot; notch ribbon ends. Glue knot to overlap of ribbon on basket. Fill basket with shredded paper. Fill plastic bag with crackers. Tie top of bag with ribbon scrap. Place cheese ball and crackers in basket.

Fig. 1

Fig. 2

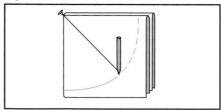

*G*ive a Christmas tree that is also a great advent calendar. Kids will love to pull off one candy a day to count down to Christmas. Simply tie 25 candies to the tree for a sweet reminder each day in December.

SANTA CANDY

- 3 ounces chocolate candy coating
- 3 ounces white candy coating

In separate small saucepans, melt white candy coating and chocolate candy coating over low heat, stirring constantly. Using a spoon, fill 7 ungreased 1-inch Santa candy molds with chocolate candy coating. Place molds in freezer until candy coating hardens. Press on back of molds to remove candies. Repeat procedure with white candy coating. Store in an airtight container. *Yield:* about 14 candies

CANDY CHRISTMAS TREE

You will need a 5" x 24" piece of red-and-white striped fabric, needle and thread, 24" tabletop Christmas tree, variety of colored cellophane, and thin gold ribbon.

1. For tree skirt, hem all raw edges of fabric by folding edges under ⅛" twice and stitching with hemstitch. Stitch two rows of basting stitches ½" and ⅝" from one long edge. Pull threads to gather fabric around base of tree; tie thread ends together to hold gathers.
2. Referring to photo, wrap individual candies in pieces of colored cellophane. Tie ribbon into a bow around top of each. Tie each candy to tree branch with another piece of ribbon.

77

RECIPE COLLECTION

Treat a special friend to a batch of these delightful brownies along with a pretty recipe book. Be sure to include the recipe for these brownies— she'll want to make more when these are gone!

BUTTERSCOTCH BROWNIES

- 1 cup butter or margarine
- 1 package (11 ounces) butterscotch chips, divided
- 4 eggs
- 1 cup granulated sugar
- 1 cup firmly packed brown sugar
- 2 cups all-purpose flour
- ½ teaspoon salt
- 1 teaspoon vanilla-butter-nut flavoring
- 1 teaspoon vanilla extract
- 1½ cups chopped pecans, toasted

Preheat oven to 325 degrees. Line a 9 x 13-inch baking pan with aluminum foil over ends of pan; grease foil. In a small saucepan over low heat, melt butter and 1 cup butterscotch chips. Cool while mixing other ingredients. In a large bowl, add eggs and beat well. Gradually add sugars, beating until well blended. In a small bowl, combine flour and salt. Add flour mixture to egg mixture. Stir in vanilla-butter-nut flavoring and vanilla. Stir in melted butter mixture, remaining butterscotch chips, and pecans. Spread batter into prepared pan. Bake 40 to 45 minutes or until top is golden brown and brownies pull away from sides of pan. Cool in pan on a wire rack. Use ends of foil to lift brownies from pan. Cut into 2-inch squares. Store in an airtight container.
Yield: about 24 brownies

CHRISTMAS RECIPES BOOK

You will need a 6½" photo album with binder clip, spray adhesive, 6½" x 14½" piece of batting, 8½" x 16½" piece of fabric, hot glue gun, 24" of ½"w ribbon, watercolor paper, gold spray paint (optional), handmade paper (optional), and recipe cards.

1. Remove photo pages from album. Open album flat so that outside is faceup. Lightly spray outside of album with spray adhesive. Adhere batting piece to sprayed album.
2. Center album, batting side down, on wrong side of fabric. Use hot glue to glue side edges of fabric to inside of album. If necessary, trim fabric that will be folded up next to binder clip. Fold long top and bottom edges to inside of album and hot glue in place, folding corners as you would a package so fabric lies flat.
3. Cut ribbon in half. Center and hot glue one end of one ribbon to one side edge of album (Fig. 1). Repeat with remaining ribbon half and remaining side edge of album.
4. Measure and cut pieces of watercolor paper equal to inside front cover of album, inside back cover of album, and small pieces for spine to fit between top and bottom edges of album and binder clip.
5. If desired, barely pressing on nozzle of gold spray paint so that paint spits out in spurts and dots, spatter paint one side of each watercolor piece. Allow to dry. Coat unpainted side of watercolor paper pieces with spray adhesive. Center corresponding pieces on inside of album and press into place, covering raw edges of fabric and ends of ribbons.
6. Put photo pages back into album. Write recipe for Butterscotch Brownies on handmade paper or recipe card. Insert paper or card into first page of album.

Fig. 1

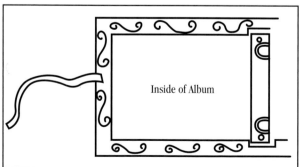

Inside of Album

CANDY CUTOUTS

*T*his treat celebrates the best of both worlds: it's a candy and a cookie! Use your favorite Christmas cookie cutters to create fun shapes to fill with red and green candies. The wooden tray can be used for serving hot cocoa and all kinds of holiday sweets.

CANDY CUTOUT COOKIES

  1   cup butter or margarine, softened
  1   cup granulated sugar
  2   eggs
  1   teaspoon vanilla extract
  3⅓ cup all-purpose flour
  1   teaspoon baking powder
  ½   teaspoon salt
      Vegetable cooking spray
  1   cup each of green and red finely
      crushed hard candies (about 40
      candies of each color)

For cookies, cream butter and sugar in a large bowl until fluffy. Add eggs and vanilla; beat until smooth. In a medium bowl, stir together flour, baking powder, and salt. Add dry ingredients to creamed mixture; stir until soft dough forms. Cover and refrigerate 1 hour.

Preheat oven to 350 degrees. On a lightly floured surface, use a floured rolling pin to roll out dough to ¼-inch thickness. Use 2¼-inch round cookie cutters to cut out cookies. Transfer cookies to foil-lined baking sheet sprayed with cooking spray, leaving 1 inch between cookies. Use Christmas-shaped aspic cutters to cut out designs from center of each cookie. Sprinkle some centers with crushed red candies and some with green. Bake 8 to 10 minutes or until cookies are

firm. Cool completely on foil. Carefully remove cookies from foil. Store in an airtight container.
Yield: about 4½ dozen cookies

PAINTED TRAY

Allow paint and sealer to dry after each application.

You will need a paintbrush, white acrylic paint, sponge stamps in desired shapes, natural finish wooden tray, non-toxic clear acrylic spray sealer, and 1"w sheer ribbon (optional).

1. Using paintbrush, paint coat of white acrylic paint on sponge side of stamps. Stamp surface of tray as desired, reloading sponge with paint as needed.
2. Spray coat of acrylic sealer over painted surface of tray. Then spray second coat of acrylic sealer on tray.
3. If desired, stack several cookies and tie with length of sheer ribbon. Repeat to make additional cookie stacks as desired.

easy!

THE GIFT OF GRANOLA

*S*weetened dried cranberries give this granola a Christmas look. Just combine ingredients and bake for a healthy snack. The rickrack-embellished jar adds a bit of old-fashioned charm to the gift.

GRANOLA MIX

- 2 (3-ounce) packages ramen noodles
- 4 cups regular oats, uncooked
- 1 (2⅛-ounce) jar sesame seeds (⅓ cup)
- 1 (3.75-ounce) package sunflower kernels (¾ cup)
- ⅓ cup dry-roasted peanuts
- ⅓ cup firmly packed brown sugar
- ¼ cup honey
- ¼ cup vegetable oil
- 1 teaspoon vanilla extract
- ½ cup sweetened dried cranberries

Preheat oven to 325 degrees. Remove seasoning packets from noodles and reserve for other uses; break noodles into small pieces. Combine noodles, oats, sesame seeds, sunflower kernels, and peanuts in a large bowl; set aside. Combine brown sugar, honey, vegetable oil, and vanilla extract; pour over noodle mixture and stir well. Spread mixture evenly in a 10 x 15- inch jellyroll pan. Bake for 30 minutes or until golden brown, stirring mixture every 10 minutes. Stir in cranberries. Cool and store mixture in an airtight container. Serve with milk or over frozen yogurt.

Yield: about 8½ cups granola

EMBELLISHED JARS

For each jar, you will need 1 yd. of green rickrack, ½ yd. of small red rickrack, craft glue, 3½" x 5½" piece of heavyweight paper, ½" dia. yellow star button (without shank), permanent red marker, spray adhesive, wide-mouth quart-size canning jar and lid, and 4" sq. of red fabric.

1. From green rickrack, cut one each of the following: 2" piece, 1½" piece, 1" piece, and ¾" piece. From red rickrack, cut two 5½" pieces.

2. Referring to photo, glue one red rickrack piece along each long edge of piece of heavyweight paper. Referring to photo and beginning with 2" piece of green rickrack at bottom, glue green rickrack pieces in descending order to left side of paper to form Christmas tree. Glue yellow star at top of tree. Allow to dry.

3. Using red marker, write "Granola Mix" on right side of paper. Turn paper label over; apply spray adhesive to back. Adhere label to front of jar.

4. Remove lid from canning jar. Using round insert in lid as pattern, draw circle on red fabric square; cut out. Lightly apply spray adhesive to top of lid insert only. Center fabric circle over adhesive-coated lid; press fabric circle in place. Replace lid insert in lid.

5. Fill jar with gift; screw lid on jar. Tie remaining rickrack around rim of jar lid, tying ends in knot. Trim ends.

GIVE A COFFEE BREAK

*L*et busy elves enjoy coffeehouse flavor at home. This dainty tin filled with Cappuccino Mix encourages holiday shoppers to slow down. Pair the blend with cinnamon-scented coasters, and shoppers are guaranteed to feel refreshed and ready to tackle the crowds again!

CAPPUCCINO MIX

- 1 cup powdered instant non-dairy creamer
- 1 cup chocolate milk mix
- ⅔ cup instant coffee granules
- ½ cup sugar
- ½ teaspoon ground cinnamon
- ¼ teaspoon ground nutmeg

Combine all ingredients; mix well. Store in an airtight container.

To serve, place 1 tablespoon plus 1 teaspoon mix in a cup. Add 1 cup boiling water; stir well.

Yield: 33 servings

AROMATIC COASTERS AND MATCHING TIN

For four coasters and one tin, you will need ⅜ yd. of Christmas print fabric; batting; thread to match fabric; six tablespoons whole cloves; four cinnamon sticks, broken into small pieces; hand-sewing needle; 1 yd. of 1¼"w wire-edged sheer ribbon; 3 yds. of thin gold ribbon; artificial berries, such as amaranthus; small plain white tin; 1"w bristle paintbrush; acrylic paints in colors to match fabric; 2½" x 4" piece of paper; and 1 yd. of ½"w gold ribbon.

Allow paint to dry after each application.

1. For coasters, from fabric, cut eight 6½" squares. From batting, cut four 6½" squares. For each coaster, layer two fabric squares, right sides matching; top with batting square. Using ¼" seam allowance, stitch along sides, leaving 2" opening for turning; trim batting close to stitching.

Trim corners, turn, and press. Combine cloves and cinnamon stick pieces. Spoon approximately 1½ tablespoons of spice mixture into coaster. Slipstitch opening closed.

2. Tie stack of coasters together with sheer ribbon and thin gold ribbon. Tuck artificial berries into ribbons.

3. For tin, using dry paintbrush and acrylic paints, paint feathery brushstrokes on sides of tin and lid.

4. Fold 2½" x 4" piece of paper in half. Using same technique, paint brushstrokes on front of folded card. Write serving instructions on inside of card. Using sewing needle, poke hole in top corner of card.

5. Fill tin with gift. Place lid on tin. Tie tin with ½"w gold ribbon and thin gold ribbon. Tuck artificial berries in ribbons. Use additional thin gold ribbon to attach card to container.

ALMOND ANGEL

A basketful of Almond Meringues is truly an angelic gift. These cookies are an airy snack between heavy holiday meals. Give the cookies away quickly; they become chewy with storage.

ALMOND MERINGUES

2   cups slivered almonds, toasted
2   cups confectioners sugar
3   egg whites
1   tablespoon amaretto
1   teaspoon almond extract
¼   teaspoon salt

Preheat oven to 300 degrees. Line baking sheet with parchment paper. Process almonds and confectioners sugar in a large food processor until almonds are finely ground. In a large bowl, combine egg whites, amaretto, almond extract, and salt. Beat until stiff peaks form. Gradually fold almond mixture into egg white mixture. Drop teaspoonfuls of batter onto prepared baking sheet. Bake 12 to 15 minutes or until cookies are lightly browned. Turn oven off and leave door closed 15 minutes. Transfer cookies to a wire rack to cool. Store in an airtight container.
Yield: about 5½ dozen cookies

ANGEL ORNAMENT BASKET

You will need embroidery floss (see color key, page 133), 5" x 9" piece of white Aida (14 ct), cardboard, low-loft batting, hot glue gun, 15½" of gold braid, basket (we used an 8" x 12" oval basket), 30" of 1½"w sheer ribbon, and fabric.

Refer to Cross Stitch, page 154, before beginning project.

1. Using three strands of floss for *Cross Stitches* and one strand of floss for *Backstitches,* center and stitch design, page 133, on Aida.
2. Cut one 2¾" x 5" piece each from cardboard and batting. Center batting and then stitched piece on cardboard. Glue edges of stitched piece to back of cardboard. Glue braid along edges of ornament. Glue ornament to front of basket.
3. Tie ribbon into a bow; glue bow to top edge of ornament.
4. Use fabric and follow *Making a Basket Liner,* page 152, to make a liner with finished edges. Place liner and gift in basket.

FELIZ NAVIDAD!

Spice up Christmas with Apricot Salsa. Made with dried apricots and fresh tomatoes and peppers, this salsa's a colorful change from typical winter cuisine. Decorate the jar with bright ribbon and peppers for a red-hot holiday gift.

APRICOT SALSA

1	package (7 ounces) dried apricots, chopped
1¼	cups chopped yellow pepper
1½	cups seeded and chopped plum tomatoes (5 medium tomatoes)
½	cup sliced green onions
1	jalapeño pepper, seeded and chopped
5	tablespoons honey
3	tablespoons freshly squeezed lemon juice
2	tablespoons chopped fresh rosemary
½	teaspoon salt

In a medium bowl, combine all ingredients. Cover and chill salsa to let flavors blend.
Yield: about 3 cups salsa

FIESTA CONTAINER

You will need a 4" x 15" piece of corrugated cardboard, one-liter clamp top jar, jute twine, red raffia, hot glue gun, dried evergreen, artificial jalapeño peppers, red paper, scrap of green paper, craft glue, black permanent fine-point marker, and a hole punch.

1. Wrap corrugated cardboard around jar until short cut ends just meet at front of jar. Tie jute twine around top and bottom edges of cardboard to secure. Tie several lengths of raffia into a bow around center of cardboard.

2. Hot glue evergreen sprigs to top of jar lid. Hot glue several artificial jalapeño peppers on top of evergreen sprigs. Holding several lengths of jute twine and raffia as one, tie lengths into a bow. Hot glue bow on top of evergreen sprig ends.

3. Transfer jalapeño pepper pattern, page 150, to red paper; cut out. Transfer jalapeño pepper stem pattern to green paper; cut out. Use craft glue to glue stem to top of pepper; allow to dry. Use black marker to outline stem and pepper. Write "Feliz Navidad!" on front of pepper. Punch hole in top of pepper. Fill jar with gift. Replace lid. Use length of jute twine to tie jalapeño pepper tag to jar.

HOME FOR THE HOLIDAYS

*P*resent these house-shaped *Peanut Butter-Cocoa Cookies packed in a homespun gift bag to friends and neighbors.*

PEANUT BUTTER-COCOA COOKIES

- ½ cup butter or margarine, softened
- ½ cup smooth peanut butter
- 1 cup granulated sugar
- ¾ cup firmly packed brown sugar
- 1 egg
- 1 teaspoon vanilla extract
- 1 cup all-purpose flour
- ½ cup cocoa
- ¼ teaspoon salt

In a large bowl, cream butter, peanut butter, and sugars until fluffy. Add egg and vanilla; beat until smooth. In a small bowl, combine flour, cocoa, and salt. Add dry ingredients to creamed mixture; stir until a soft dough forms. Divide dough in half; cover and chill 2 hours.

Preheat oven to 375 degrees. On a lightly floured surface, use a floured rolling pin to roll out dough to ⅛-inch thickness. Use a 4 x 3-inch house-shaped cookie cutter to cut out cookies. Place 2 inches apart on a greased baking sheet. Use a 1⅛-inch heart-shaped cookie cutter to cut out a heart in center of each cookie. Bake 5 to 7 minutes or until edges are firm. Transfer cookies to a wire rack to cool. Store in an airtight container.

Yield: about 2 dozen cookies

APPLIQUÉD HOME BAG

You will need a 4" x 3" house-shaped cookie cutter, 1⅛" heart-shaped cookie cutter, paper-backed fusible web, fabric, red felt, 5¼" x 8½" brown gift bag with handles, hot glue gun, one ½" dia. and one ¾" dia. buttons, black permanent fine-point marker, wood-tone spray, photocopy of tag design (page 149) on white card stock, and several 20" lengths of raffia.

1. Use cookie cutters and follow *Making Appliqués,* page 153, to make one house appliqué in reverse from fabric and one heart appliqué from felt. Fuse house to bag; then fuse heart to house. Glue ½" dia. button to heart.

2. Use marker to draw "stitches" on bag along house lines.

3. Apply wood-tone spray to front of bag; allow to dry. Cut out tag; glue above house.

4. Tie raffia into a bow. Glue bow to bag and remaining button to knot of bow.

SNACK WITH A TWIST

*T*wist up the flavor of a favorite crunchy snack with garlic and cumin. A cobra basket is the perfect container for presenting the spicy gift. Warn recipients that the pretzels pack quite a bite!

SOUTHWESTERN PRETZELS

 1 package (10 ounces) Bavarian-style hard pretzels
 3 tablespoons butter or margarine
 ½ teaspoon ground cumin
 ½ teaspoon chili powder
 ½ teaspoon garlic powder

Preheat oven to 225 degrees. Place pretzels in a single layer on a baking sheet. In a small saucepan, melt butter over medium-low heat. Add cumin, chili powder, and garlic powder; stir until well blended. Brush butter mixture over top of each pretzel. Bake 18 to 22 minutes or until dry to the touch. Cool on baking sheet. Store in an airtight container. *Yield:* about 20 pretzels

GIFT-WRAPPED COBRA BASKET

You will need a gift box-style basket with lid (we used a 7" sq. basket), 2"w wired ribbon, hot glue gun, 1¾" dia. jingle bell, ¹⁄₁₆" dia. gold cord, and one 24" length each of ⅛"w and ¼"w satin ribbons.

1. Beginning at rim and measuring under basket to opposite rim, measure basket (Fig. 1); add 8". Cut two lengths of wired ribbon the determined measurement. Wrapping ribbon ends to inside of box, arrange ribbon around box; glue to secure.

Fig. 1

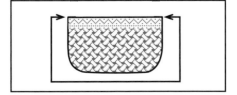

2. In same manner, measure lid top rim to rim; add 6". Cut two lengths of wired ribbon the determined measurement. Wrapping ribbon ends to inside of lid, arrange ribbon around lid; glue to secure. 3. Tie a 24" length of wired ribbon into a bow. Thread jingle bell onto cord. Use cord and satin ribbons to attach bow to ribbons on lid; tie cord and ribbons into a bow.

HEAVENLY TREAT

*L*et a friend know she's heaven sent with an angelic
thank-you gift! A paper-bag angel carries a jar of Heavenly Dessert
Topping, a tropical treat that's dreamy served with cake or ice cream.
Be sure to include a loaf of angel food cake in your gift basket.

HEAVENLY DESSERT TOPPING

1   can (20 ounces) crushed
      pineapple in heavy syrup,
      undrained
¾   cup sugar
2   tablespoons cornstarch
½   cup flaked coconut
½   cup chopped macadamia nuts
      Angel food cake to serve, optional

Combine pineapple, sugar, and cornstarch in a medium saucepan. Stirring constantly, cook over medium heat until mixture boils (about 8 minutes). Remove from heat. Stir in coconut and macadamia nuts. Serve warm over cake or ice cream. Store in an airtight container in refrigerator.
Yield: about 3 cups topping

ANGEL BAG AND BASKET

You will need a 2" dia. plastic foam ball, sandal-foot nylon stocking, hot glue gun, curly doll hair, black permanent fine-point marker, cosmetic blush, craft stick, fabric, white lunch-size paper bag, decorative-edge craft scissors, heart-motif rubber stamp, ink pad, 5" of white chenille stem, basket (we used a 8" x 11" white basket with handle), tracing paper, poster board, and craft glue.

Allow craft glue to dry after each application.

1. For angel head, place ball in toe of stocking. Gather stocking smoothly around ball; hot glue gathers to secure. Trim stocking close to gathers.
2. Arrange and hot glue hair on head. Use marker to draw eyes and mouth. Use blush to add cheeks. Insert 1" of craft stick into bottom of head. Tear a ½" x 5" piece from fabric; tie into a bow and hot glue to craft stick under head.
3. Trim top of bag with decorative-edge scissors. With bag closed, starting at top of bag, stamp hearts along bottom front of bag. Cut 4" down center front and back of bag.
4. Place gift in bag. Gather bag at bottom of cut; secure with chenille stem. Spread top of bag open to shape wings. Insert craft stick under head through center of gathers.
5. For basket liner, use fabric and follow *Making a Basket Liner,* page 152, to make a liner with unfinished edges. Place liner and bag in basket.
6. For tag, trace pattern, page 138, onto tracing paper; cut out. Using pattern, cut one heart shape from fabric. Draw around pattern twice on poster board; cut out. Using craft glue, glue fabric heart to one poster board heart; trim edges with craft scissors. Trim ¼" from all sides of remaining poster board heart. Use craft glue to glue small heart to center of fabric heart. Use marker to draw dots and "stitches" along edges of small heart and to write message on tag. Hot glue tag to front of basket.

ORANGE LIQUEUR SAUCE

*T*his sauce, made with liqueur and a sugar syrup, enhances the flavor of turkey or ham. After the sauce is gone, the gilded jar becomes a storage container pretty enough to stay on the counter.

CREAMY ORANGE LIQUEUR SAUCE

  ½ cup water
  ½ cup granulated sugar
  ½ cup firmly packed brown sugar
  1 cup whipping cream
  ⅓ cup orange-flavored liqueur

In a heavy large saucepan, combine water and sugars. Stirring constantly, cook over medium-low heat until sugars dissolve. Increase heat to medium-high. Stirring frequently, cook about 9 minutes or until mixture turns a dark golden brown and has reduced almost by half its volume. Remove from heat. Whisking constantly, very slowly add whipping cream to caramel mixture. Place on medium-low heat. Stirring frequently, cook 20 minutes or until sauce thickens. Remove from heat. Stir in liqueur. Store in an airtight container in refrigerator. Serve at room temperature.
Yield: about 1⅔ cups sauce

BEADED FRUIT JAR

You will need a clear glass jar with wooden lid with rubber stopper, gold spray webbing, hot glue gun, artificial velvet leaves, 1 yd. of ⅜"-wide burgundy grosgrain ribbon, miniature beaded fruit, gift tag, hole punch, and ¼"w satin ribbon.

1. Remove lid from jar and set aside. Lightly spray outside of jar with spray webbing; allow to dry.
2. Glue velvet leaves to top of lid, letting points of leaves drape over sides of lid. Cut 6" length from ribbon. With remaining length of ribbon, make multiple loops. Tie center of loops with reserved 6" length of ribbon. Glue multi-looped bow to lid on top of leaves. Glue miniature beaded fruits to top of lid, nestling fruits between loops of bow.
3. Fill jar with gift. Replace lid on jar. Write serving directions on inside of gift tag. Punch hole in top corner of gift tag. Attach gift tag to jar with ¼"w satin ribbon.

NEW YEAR'S TRUFFLES

*R*ing in the new year on a delicious note with Chocolate Marble Truffles. Just swirl white and dark chocolate together to create confections you'll remember long after January. Place the truffles in a mini loaf pan and tie with ribbon for a presentation you'll want to toast with champagne.

CHOCOLATE MARBLE TRUFFLES

DARK CHOCOLATE
  3 (4-ounce) semisweet chocolate bars, broken into pieces
  ¼ cup whipping cream
  3 tablespoons butter, cut up
  2 tablespoons almond liqueur
WHITE CHOCOLATE
  3 (4-ounce) white chocolate bars, broken into pieces
  ¼ cup whipping cream
  3 tablespoons butter, cut up
  2 tablespoons almond liqueur
COATING (optional)
  1 bag cream-filled chocolate sandwich cookies, finely crushed

For dark chocolate mixture, microwave chocolate and whipping cream in a 2-quart microwave-safe bowl on medium power (50%) 3½ minutes. Whisk until chocolate melts and mixture is smooth. (If chocolate doesn't melt completely, microwave and whisk at 15 second intervals until melted.) Whisk in butter and liqueur.

For white chocolate mixture, repeat procedure for dark chocolate, substituting white chocolate bars for semisweet chocolate bars.

For marble truffles, spoon chocolate and

white chocolate mixtures into an 8 x 8-inch pan; swirl with a knife. Cover and chill at least 4 hours. Scooping with a melon baller, shape mixture into 1-inch balls. Roll balls in cream-filled chocolate sandwich cookie crumbs, if desired. Cover and chill up to 1 week or freeze up to 1 month.
Yield: about 2 dozen truffles

TRUFFLE CONTAINERS

For each loaf pan, you will need two silver miniature paper party cups, 3½" x 10" piece of parchment paper, 2½" x 4¼" mini loaf pan, 12" of 1¼"w silver ribbon, 16" of 1"w blue sheer ribbon, 16" of ⅛"w wired silver ribbon, and a

miniature acrylic champagne glass.

Each loaf pan will hold two truffles.

1. Place one truffle in each paper party cup. Centering parchment paper, line mini loaf pan with parchment paper. Place truffles side by side in lined mini loaf pan. Fold ends of parchment paper over truffles.
2. Tie 1¼"w silver ribbon around loaf pan; tie in knot. Trim ribbon ends. Tie 1"w blue sheer ribbon around loaf pan on top of silver ribbon; tie into a bow. Trim ribbon ends. Using ⅛"w silver ribbon, tie champagne glass to knots in ribbons. Wrap ends of ⅛"w silver ribbon around a pencil to curl.

BREAK INTO THE NEW YEAR

*O*riental Cashew Brittle throws quite a surprise for a New Year's Eve party. Ginger, red pepper, five-spice powder, and cashews add a new sensation to an old temptation.

ORIENTAL CASHEW BRITTLE

1½ cups sugar
½ cup light corn syrup
¼ cup water
2 cups cashews
1½ tablespoons butter
1 teaspoon Chinese five-spice powder
½ teaspoon salt
¼ teaspoon ground ginger
⅛ teaspoon ground red pepper
1 teaspoon baking soda

Butter sides of a heavy saucepan. Combine sugar, corn syrup, and water in saucepan. Stirring constantly, cook over medium-low heat until sugar dissolves. Using a pastry brush dipped in hot water, wash down any sugar crystals on sides of pan. Attach a candy thermometer to pan, making sure thermometer does not touch bottom of pan. Increase heat to medium and bring to a boil. Cook, without stirring, until syrup reaches hard-crack stage (approximately 300 to 310 degrees) and turns light golden in color. Test about ½ teaspoon syrup in ice water. Syrup will form brittle threads in ice water and will remain brittle when removed from water. Remove from heat and stir in cashews, butter, five-spice powder, salt, ginger, and red pepper; stir until butter melts. Add baking soda (syrup will foam); stir until soda dissolves. Pour syrup onto a large piece of buttered aluminum foil; cool

completely. Break into pieces. Store in an airtight container.
Yield: about 1½ pounds candy

BRITTLE PACKAGING

You will need one sheet iridescent cellophane, 1 yd. of 1¼"w black sheer ribbon, silver writing pen, 2" x 3" piece of black paper, hole punch, and a decorative pair of chopsticks.

1. Center gift on cellophane. Gather cellophane around gift. Tie ribbon into a bow around cellophane. Trim cellophane and ribbon ends if necessary.
2. Using silver pen, write message on black paper. Punch hole in upper left corner of black paper. Thread card onto one free end of ribbon. Slip pair of chopsticks through knot in bow.

HEARTFELT SWEETS

Give someone special a little piece of your heart with these irresistible cakes. A touch of orange liqueur lends rich flavor to the frosting, which is topped with a dark chocolate glaze. Enclose the sweets in a wrapped box finished with a flower-topped ribbon.

CHOCOLATE-GRAND MARNIER HEARTS

CAKE
- 1 package (18¼ ounces) devil's food cake mix and ingredients to prepare cake
- 2 tablespoons Grand Marnier liqueur

ORANGE CREAM FROSTING
- ⅓ cup butter or margarine, softened
- 2 tablespoons orange juice
- 1 teaspoon grated orange zest
- ⅛ teaspoon salt
- 4 cups confectioners sugar
- ¼ cup Grand Marnier liqueur

CHOCOLATE GLAZE
- 5 ounces bittersweet baking chocolate, chopped
- 3 tablespoons vegetable shortening

Preheat oven to 350 degrees. For cake, grease and line two 10½ x 15½-inch jellyroll pans with waxed paper; grease waxed paper. In a large bowl, prepare cake mix according to package directions, stirring in liqueur. Spread batter into prepared pans. Bake 10 to 12 minutes or until a toothpick inserted in center of each cake comes out clean. Let cool completely in pans. Invert cakes onto a flat surface and remove waxed paper.

For orange cream frosting, beat butter, orange juice, orange zest, and salt in a

medium bowl until fluffy. Gradually add confectioners sugar; beat until well blended. Add liqueur, 1 tablespoon at a time, beating until smooth. Spread frosting over cooled cakes.

For chocolate glaze, combine chocolate and shortening in a small saucepan. Stirring constantly, cook over low heat until chocolate melts. Remove from heat. Cool 5 minutes. Pour glaze over frosting. Using a warm spatula, spread glaze evenly over cakes.

Use a 2¼-inch-wide heart-shaped metal cookie cutter to cut out cakes. (*Note:* For ease in cutting cakes, wipe cookie cutter with a paper towel between cuts.) Store in a single layer in an airtight container in refrigerator. Serve chilled or at room temperature.
Yield: about 4 dozen heart cakes

GIFT-WRAPPED BOX

You will need a box with lid (we used a 5" x 10" x 1½" box), wrapping paper, ruler, spray adhesive, craft knife, cutting mat, 1½"w ribbon, 6" of floral wire, hot glue gun, silk rosebud pick, gold permanent fine-point marker, and a purchased gift tag.

1. Remove box lid. Use wrapping paper and refer to *Covering a Box,* page 152, to cover lid. Place gift in box; replace lid.
2. Measure around box; add 3". Cut a length of ribbon the determined measurement. Knot ribbon around box. Cut a 36" length of ribbon. Using ribbon, follow *Making a Bow,* page 153, to make a bow with four 5" loops and two 7" streamers; notch ends. Use wire to attach bow to knot on box.
3. Hot glue pick under center of bow.
4. Use marker to write message on tag.

VICTORIAN VALENTINES

*P*lay Cupid on the most romantic day of the year—pass out petite bags
filled with scrumptious Raspberry Caramels. For a Victorian look, embellish
satin drawstring bags with lace, appliqués, and shiny charms.

RASPBERRY CARAMELS

  2   cups sugar
  2   cups whipping cream, divided
1½ cups light corn syrup
 ¾ cup butter or margarine
 ¼ teaspoon raspberry-flavored oil
      (used in candy making)
      Burgundy paste food coloring

Line a 10½ x 15½-inch jellyroll pan
with aluminum foil, extending foil over
ends of pan; grease foil. Butter sides of a
heavy Dutch oven.

Combine sugar, 1 cup whipping
cream, corn syrup, and butter in pan.
Stirring constantly, cook over medium-
low heat until sugar dissolves. Using a
pastry brush dipped in hot water, wash
down any sugar crystals on sides of pan.
Attach a candy thermometer to pan,
making sure thermometer does not touch
bottom of pan. Continuing to stir,
increase heat to medium and bring to a
boil. Gradually add remaining 1 cup
whipping cream. Stirring frequently
without touching sides of pan, cook until
mixture reaches firm-ball stage
(approximately 242 to 248 degrees). Test
about ½ teaspoon mixture in ice water.
Mixture will roll into a firm ball in ice
water but will flatten if pressed when

removed from water. Remove from heat
and stir in flavored oil; lightly tint
mixture. Immediately pour into prepared
pan. Cool at room temperature several
hours. Cut into 1-inch squares using a
lightly oiled knife. Wrap caramels
individually in foil candy wrappers or
waxed paper and store in a cool place.
Yield: about 11½ dozen caramels

VALENTINE BAGS

For each bag, you will need ½"w and
1"w white lace; 2"w white lace heart
appliqué; 4½" x 5½" red fabric bag with
drawstrings; seam ripper; 4mm dark
pink, green, and pink silk ribbons; pink
embroidery floss; chenille needle; hot
glue gun; gold charm; red sewing thread;
beading needle; red frosted glass seed
beads; 2¼" x 3¼" piece of pink card
stock; decorative-edge craft scissors;
1¼" x 1¾" self-adhesive Valentine-motif
sticker; and a hole punch.

*Refer to Embroidery Stitches and
Ribbon Embroidery Stitches, pages 154
and 155, before beginning project. Work
all embroidery stitches through one
layer of bag only.*

1. Arrange lace and heart on front of bag.
Use seam ripper to remove a few stitches
at seam line to insert ends of lace into
seam. Stitch openings closed. Repeat to
stitch lace to back of bag, if desired. Stitch
heart to bag.
2. Using dark pink ribbon, floss, and
chenille needle, work a *Spiderweb Rose,*
page 155, at center of heart. Use green
ribbon to work three *Lazy Daisy Stitches,*
page 155, for leaves around rose. Tie 5"
of pink ribbon into a bow. Glue bow and
charm to heart.
3. Use pink ribbon to work *Running
Stitches,* page 155, through center
of ½"w lace. Use red thread and beading
needle to sew four beads between
each stitch.
4. For each bud on 1"w lace, use pink
ribbon to work *French Knots,* page 155,
and green ribbon to work *Japanese
Ribbon Stitches,* page 155, on each side
of knot.
5. For tag, match short edges and fold
card stock in half. Use decorative-edge
scissors to trim edges of tag. Apply sticker
to front of tag. Punch hole in corner of
tag. Remove knot from drawstring at one
side of bag; thread tag onto drawstring
and retie knot.

MARDI GRAS MADNESS

A Mardi Gras celebration wouldn't be complete without pralines. These sweets are made in the microwave, so they're both quick and easy. For an authentic New Orleans look, give the pralines in small colorful beaded bags.

MICROWAVE PRALINES

- 2 cups sugar
- 2 cups pecans
- 1 (5-ounce) can evaporated milk
- ¼ cup butter or margarine
- 1 tablespoon vanilla extract

Combine all ingredients in a 2-quart glass liquid measuring cup. Microwave on high power 5 to 6 minutes (see Note), stirring well with a wooden spoon. Microwave 5 to 6 minutes more, stirring well. Working rapidly, drop by tablespoonfuls onto waxed paper; let stand until firm.
Yield: about 30 pralines
Note: If your oven is 1000 watts or more, use the lower time option.

MARDI GRAS BAGS

For each bag, you will need two 4" x 5" pieces of felt, thread to match felt, flexible wire, variety of small shiny beads, needle-nose pliers, and coordinating waxed tissue paper.

1. To make bag, pin felt pieces together; leaving ¼" seam allowance, stitch along sides and bottom. Fold bottom seam to meet side seams and stitch across corners to create flat bottom on bag (Fig. 1). Trim corners, leaving ¼" seam allowance. Turn right side out.
2. Cut a 14" length of wire. Using wire as

Fig. 1

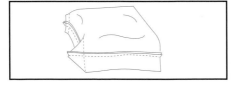

you would a needle and thread, "stitch" wire around top edge of bag, actually

punching wire through felt and stringing beads onto wire as you go. Use needle-nose pliers to make decorative twists in wire as desired. Use pliers to trim ends of wire if needed and to twist wire ends together to secure.
3. Line bag with tissue paper. Place gift inside bag.

TOP O' THE MORNING!

*O*ur St. Patrick's Day Candy
Mix offers a sweet way to celebrate
the annual wearing of the green. For
good luck, deliver a bag of the blend
in a tiny top hat with a shamrock
name tag.

ST. PATRICK'S DAY CANDY MIX

1½ pounds small green gourmet jelly
      beans (about 3 cups)
  2 cans (6 ounces each) roasted and
      salted whole almonds
  1 package (8 ounces) yogurt-
      covered raisins

In a medium bowl, combine jelly beans,
almonds, and raisins. Store in an airtight
container.
Yield: about 5 cups candy mix

SHAMROCK TAGS AND TOP HATS

For each tag, you will need tracing paper,
green card stock, gold glitter dimensional
paint, black permanent fine-point marker,
hot glue gun, 3½" craft pick, transparent
tape, small green plastic top hat, small plastic
bag, and green and gold curling ribbon.

1. Trace shamrock pattern, page 136, onto
tracing paper; cut out. Draw around
pattern on card stock; cut out.
2. Use dimensional paint to outline edges
of shamrock. Use marker to write message
on tag. Glue pick to back of shamrock.
Tape pick to inside of top hat.
3. Fill bag with gift. Tie top of bag with
curling ribbon. Place gift in top hat.

EGGS-CLUSIVELY FOR EASTER!

Even the Easter Bunny couldn't make eggs better than these extremely rich and chocolaty treats. The eggs should chill overnight, so start your work early. Little girls will adore the painted egg box; it's just right for storing hairbows and ribbons.

CHOCOLATE-COATED EASTER EGGS

½   cup butter, softened
¼   cup evaporated milk
5   cups sifted powdered sugar
1   teaspoon vanilla extract
1   (3½-ounce) can flaked coconut
1   cup chopped toasted pecans
12   ounces chocolate candy coating
1   (16-ounce) can homestyle vanilla
     frosting (optional)
16   paper baking cups

Beat butter at medium speed of an electric mixer until fluffy. Add milk; gradually add sugar, beating well. Stir in vanilla, coconut, and pecans. Cover and chill overnight. Divide mixture into 16 equal portions. Shape each portion into an oval with a flat bottom; place on waxed paper-lined baking sheet and chill thoroughly. Melt chocolate candy coating over low heat, stirring constantly. Carefully dip bottom of each oval in candy coating. Place ovals, coated side down, on waxed paper-lined baking sheet; chill 15 minutes. Place ovals on a wire rack over waxed paper. Spoon remaining candy coating over ovals, letting excess candy coating drip onto waxed paper. If desired, place vanilla frosting in a zip-top plastic bag. Pierce the bag with a toothpick and pipe the frosting over eggs to decorate. Chill eggs on a wire rack 15 minutes or until firm. Store eggs in paper baking cups in an airtight container in refrigerator.
Yield: 16 (1-ounce) eggs

EASTER EGG BOX

You will need an oval papier-mâché box; ¼" flat paintbrush; 1" flat paintbrush; rose pink, white, purple, blue, yellow, and bright pink acrylic paint; clear acrylic spray sealer; and excelsior.

Allow paint and sealer to dry after each application.

1. Using a pencil, lightly draw an arched line on top center of box lid. Using 1" brush, paint one half of top of lid rose pink; paint other half white. Then paint rim of box lid and bottom of box white.
2. Referring to photo and using ¼" brush and white paint, paint a line of rickrack on rose pink area of box lid. Using same brush and purple and blue paints, paint stylized flowers on top of lid as desired. Dip handle of paintbrush in yellow paint and paint a dot in center of each flower; paint additional dots scattered over top of box lid.
3. Referring to photo and using ¼" brush and bright pink paint, paint checkerboard around rim of box lid. Using 1" brush and yellow paint, paint stripes around sides of box bottom. Using ¼" brush and bright pink paint, paint a line of rickrack around bottom of box bottom.
4. Spray entire box with coat of acrylic sealer. Fill box with excelsior. Place chocolate eggs in box.

TIPSY BERRY SAUCE

Take advantage of the fruits of summer! Blended with blackberries and brandy, this Tipsy Berry Sauce really packs a punch. Drizzle the sauce over ice cream or cake for a dessert folks will remember. Dress up the jar with a handmade paper lid and tie on raffia and a berry pick.

TIPSY BERRY SAUCE

2   packages (12 ounces each) frozen whole blackberries, thawed
½   cup blackberry-flavored brandy
1   cup sugar
2   tablespoons cornstarch

In a medium bowl, combine blackberries and brandy. Let stand at room temperature 2 hours, stirring occasionally.

In a medium saucepan, combine blackberry mixture, sugar, and cornstarch. Stirring constantly, bring to a boil over medium-high heat. Cook until mixture thickens and is no longer cloudy (about 3 minutes). Store in an airtight container in refrigerator. Serve chilled over ice cream or cake.
Yield: about 3¾ cups sauce

TIPSY TOPPER

You will need a half-pint jar with lid, handmade paper, decorative-edge craft scissors, green raffia, artificial berry pick with leaves, footed dessert dish, and excelsior.

1. Remove lid from jar. Draw around jar lid on wrong side of paper; then use decorative-edge scissors to cut out circle 1" outside drawn line.
2. Fill jar with sauce; replace lid on jar. Center paper circle over lid; knot raffia around lid to secure. Tuck stem of berry pick under knot of raffia.
3. Line dessert dish with excelsior. Place gift in dish.

PINEAPPLE REFRESHER

*A*dd spirit to any occasion with an offering of our elegant Pineapple Cordial. Pour the sweet potable into a decorative ribbon-tied bottle. Then pack the fruity tidbits in a jar and add a beaded doily topper.

PINEAPPLE CORDIAL

- 2 cups sugar
- 2 cups water
- 1 package (6 ounces) dried pineapple
- 1 bottle (750 ml) vodka

In a medium saucepan, combine sugar, water, and pineapple. Stirring constantly, bring to a boil over medium heat. Remove from heat; cool. Pour pineapple mixture into a 2-quart container. Stir in vodka. Cover and store in a cool place 3 weeks to let flavors blend.

Reserving pineapple, strain cordial into gift bottles. Place pineapple pieces in a jar with lid. Store in refrigerator. Serve cordial with pineapple.

Yield: about 5 cups cordial

DOILY LID COVER AND BOW

You will need white spray primer; jar with lid; white acrylic paint; paintbrush; beading needle; clear, navy, and gold seed beads; gold and gold frosted E beads; white sewing thread; 6" dia. white doily; ¼"w satin ribbon; ⅞"w sheer wired ribbon; glass bottle with lid; 8" of craft wire; hot glue gun; artificial small flower pick with leaves; purchased bucket; and shredded paper.

Allow primer and paint to dry after each application.

1. Remove lid from jar. Apply primer to jar lid; then paint lid white.
2. Using beading needle, refer to Fig. 1 to make twelve beaded dangles.
3. Use thread to attach dangles at 1½" intervals around edges of doily.
4. Fill jar with pineapple; replace lid. Center doily over lid. Thread satin ribbon through holes in doily around lid; tie into a bow.
5. Knot a length of wired ribbon around bottle. Cut a 42" length of wired ribbon. Using wired ribbon, follow *Making a Bow*, page 153, to make a bow with two 6" loops, two 5" loops, two 4" loops, and two 6" streamers. Use wire to attach bow to ribbon on bottle. Glue flower pick to bow. Line bucket with shredded paper. Place gifts in bucket.

Fig. 1

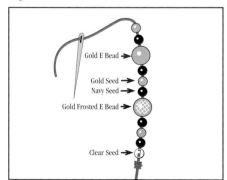

Gold E Bead

Gold Seed
Navy Seed
Gold Frosted E Bead

Clear Seed

OUT-OF-THE-ORDINARY LOAF

Layers of mouthwatering fresh asparagus, mushrooms, and melted cheese hide inside our asparagus loaf. Slice and serve it for a light lunch or as a side dish with any meal. For giving, wrap the dish in a padded fabric caddy labeled with a pretty handmade tag.

READY-TO-BAKE ASPARAGUS LOAF

1 pound fresh asparagus, trimmed and cut into 4-inch pieces
1 package (8 ounces) fresh mushrooms, sliced
2 garlic cloves, minced
1 tablespoon olive oil
1½ cups (6 ounces) finely shredded Swiss cheese, divided
¼ cup chopped fresh dill weed
1 loaf (16 ounces) unsliced French bread
4 eggs
1½ cups half and half
2 teaspoons lemon pepper
1 teaspoon salt
  Fresh dill sprig to decorate

In a large saucepan, cook asparagus in boiling water 1 minute; drain and rinse in cold water. Pat dry on paper towels; set aside. In a medium skillet over medium heat, sauté mushrooms and garlic in oil until liquid evaporates (about 6 minutes); set aside. In a medium bowl, combine 1 cup cheese and dill weed. Remove crust from bread. Slice bread lengthwise into 3 slices; trim each slice to about 3½ x 8 inches. Place 1 bread slice in bottom of a greased 4½ x 8½-inch baking dish. Place a single layer of asparagus crosswise in baking dish. Layer half of mushroom mixture and half of cheese mixture on asparagus. Repeat layers with 1 bread slice and remaining asparagus, mushroom mixture, and cheese mixture. Place remaining bread slice on top. In a medium bowl, beat eggs, half and half, lemon pepper, and salt. Slowly pour egg mixture over bread. Sprinkle with remaining ½ cup cheese. Decorate with fresh dill. Cover and refrigerate overnight. Give with baking and serving instructions.
Yield: 1 loaf

To bake and serve: Remove loaf from refrigerator 1 hour before baking. Bake uncovered in a 325-degree oven 60 to 65 minutes or until a knife inserted in center comes out clean and top is golden brown. If top browns too quickly, cover loosely with aluminum foil. Cool uncovered on a wire rack 30 minutes. Cut into 1-inch slices and serve warm.
Yield: about 8 servings

FABRIC CADDY AND TAG

You will need cotton batting, fabric, pinking shears, needle and thread, four ⁷⁄₈" dia. buttons, photocopy of tag design (page 149) on coordinating card stock, colored pencils, glue stick, 2½" x 3¾" piece of card stock, and a black permanent fine-point marker.

1. Cut one 11" x 15" piece from cotton batting and two 11" x 15" pieces from fabric. Place fabric pieces wrong sides together. Position batting between wrong sides of fabric pieces; trim edges with pinking shears.
2. Refer to Fig. 1 to cut tabs in fabric and batting. Work *Running Stitches,* page 155, ¼" from edges to secure fabrics and batting together.
3. Position and fold short edges behind long edges to form a box. Sew one button at each corner of long sides to secure.
4. Cut out tag. Use colored pencils to color tag. Center and glue tag on card stock. Use marker to write message on tag.

Fig. 1

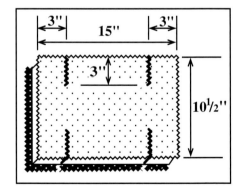

A MEMORABLE MOTHER'S DAY

*G*ive your mother a gift she'll *appreciate for months to come. She can splash a bit of Blackberry Mint Vinegar in all kinds of salad dressings and marinades. Accompany the cruet with a fresh mint plant in a painted pot, and Mom will never forget this present. Make this recipe a week before giving it away; it's best after the flavors have a chance to blend.*

BLACKBERRY-MINT VINEGAR

5	cups white vinegar (5% acidity)
2	cups fresh or frozen whole blackberries
⅓	cup sugar
⅛	teaspoon salt
8	fresh mint leaves

In a large non-aluminum saucepan, combine vinegar, blackberries, sugar, and salt. Bring to a boil over medium-high heat; boil 3 minutes. Add mint leaves. Transfer mixture to a heatproof nonmetal container. Refrigerate 5 days to let flavors blend.

Strain vinegar into gift bottles. Store in refrigerator up to 1 month.
Yield: about 5¼ cups vinegar

CRUET AND PAINT DRIP FLOWERPOT

You will need one pint each of two different coordinating colors of latex house paint, two 8" disposable baking pans, 5" to 5½" dia. clay pot, waxed paper, mint plant, sheet of heavyweight paper, decorative-edge craft scissors, wooden skewer, tape, 2 yds. of 1"w wire-edged ribbon, and a glass cruet.

1. Pour approximately ½" of base color paint in baking pan. Turn pot upside down and dip rim of pot in paint. With pot still upside down, remove pot from paint and let some of excess paint drip back into pan. Quickly turn pot right side up and set on piece of waxed paper. Allow paint to run down sides of pot and dry.

2. Fill second baking pan with approximately ½" of top color paint. As in Step 1, dip upside down pot in paint, but not quite as deeply as for first color. Repeat as in Step 1 to let paint drip and dry.

3. Plant mint in paint drip flowerpot. Using computer, or just writing freehand, make a 3" x 4" card from heavyweight paper with a Mother's Day message. Use decorative-edge scissors to trim edges of card. Break wooden skewer so it measures 6" in length. Tape top portion of skewer to back of card.

4. Cut ribbon in half. Tie one length of ribbon into a multi-looped bow around skewer at base of card. Poke skewer into soil.

5. Fill cruet with gift. Use remaining length of ribbon to tie a multi-looped bow around handle of cruet.

UNFORGETTABLE FATHER'S DAY

*M*ake this Father's Day extraordinary with Barbecued Cashews. Coated with just enough spice, these nuts won't last long. Wrap them in cellophane bags and pack them in a glittery tie box. Dad'll probably ask for these again next year—if not before.

BARBECUED CASHEWS

2	tablespoons butter or margarine
1	tablespoon white wine Worcestershire sauce
1½	tablespoons soy sauce
1	teaspoon hot sauce
½	teaspoon salt
¼	teaspoon chili powder
¼	teaspoon ground red pepper
2	cups salted cashews

Preheat oven to 350 degrees. Melt butter in a saucepan over medium heat. Stir in Worcestershire sauce and next 5 ingredients. Remove from heat. Add cashews, stirring to coat. Spread nuts in an aluminum foil-lined 10 x 15-inch jellyroll pan. Bake for 12 minutes, stirring twice. Spread nuts on paper towels; cool completely. Store in airtight container.
Yield: 2 cups cashews

TIE BOXES

For each box, you will need three different coordinating colors of tissue paper, tie box with ends that fold in, small flat paintbrush, craft glue, roll of paper crepe-type ribbon, 4" x 6" piece of heavyweight brown paper, decorative-edge craft scissors, marker in desired color, hole punch, and a clear cellophane bag.

1. Select base color of tissue paper to cover box. Crumple this piece of tissue and then flatten it on a flat surface. Unfold flaps on each end of box. Using paintbrush, apply glue to outside of box; then apply crumpled tissue to box, covering entire outside of box. Trim excess tissue.

2. Transfer desired tie pattern, page 148, to coordinating color of tissue paper and cut out. Glue tissue paper tie to front of box as shown. Cut stripes or dots from remaining color of tissue paper and glue, as desired, to front of tie as shown in photo. Referring to photo, outline tie by gluing crepe ribbon around tie shape. Allow to dry.

3. For gift tag, crumple up piece of tissue paper and then flatten. Apply glue to one side of 4" x 6" piece of paper. Apply crumpled tissue to glued side of paper; trim edges. Fold paper in half so it measures 3" x 4". Using decorative-edge scissors, cut a 2¾" x 3½" piece of coordinating color of tissue paper. Glue this piece to front of tag as shown. Using marker, write message on tag. Punch hole in upper left corner of gift tag.

4. Fill cellophane bag with gift. Tie top of bag with crepe ribbon. Thread gift tag onto one crepe ribbon end. Place gift-filled cellophane bag in tie box. Close box.

SPECIAL SAUCE FOR DAD

*D*ad will be running to light the grill when he sees this present! With a jar of Apple Barbecue Sauce adorned with a sauce mop, he won't be able to resist. Make sure to have ribs or chicken ready for him in the fridge!

APPLE BARBECUE SAUCE

- ½ cup apple jelly
- 1 (8-ounce) can tomato sauce
- ¼ cup white vinegar
- 2 tablespoons light brown sugar
- 2 tablespoons water
- 1 teaspoon hot sauce
- ¼ teaspoon salt

Bring all ingredients to a boil in a small saucepan, stirring until smooth. Reduce heat and simmer, stirring occasionally, 20 to 25 minutes. Cover and chill until ready to use.

Yield: about 1⅓ cups sauce

CRATE O' BARBECUE SAUCE

You will need a 5½" x 8" wooden crate, excelsior, 500ml glass clamp top jar, barbecue mop brush, 1 yd. of 1½"w black sheer ribbon, 1 yd. of ¾"w tartan plaid ribbon, 2" x 3¾" piece of brown paper, decorative-edge craft scissors, hole punch, black felt-tip pen, craft glue, and 8" of ⅛"w yellow satin ribbon.

1. Line wooden crate with excelsior. Fill jar with gift and clamp lid closed. Place jar on its side in wooden crate. Place mop brush beside jar.

2. Wrap sheer ribbon around center of crate and tie one-half of a knot. Cut a 1¾" length of tartan plaid ribbon. Set aside. Wrap remaining length of tartan plaid ribbon around center of crate on top of sheer ribbon. Tie plaid ribbon into a bow. Finish tying second half of knot in sheer ribbon on top of plaid ribbon.

3. For gift tag, trim edges of brown paper with decorative-edge scissors. Fold gift tag in half. Punch hole in top corner of back of tag. Write message inside tag. Glue reserved 1¾" piece of plaid ribbon across bottom half of gift tag front. Thread satin ribbon through hole in gift tag. Tie satin ribbon around knot in sheer ribbon.

NUTS ABOUT GARDENING

*S*hare a batch of simple-to-make Chocolate-Almond Macaroons with a gardening friend. Tuck the chewy treats into a handy tool caddy—the decorated wooden tote will come in handy long after the cookies are gone.

CHOCOLATE-ALMOND MACAROONS

- ½   cup semi-sweet chocolate chips
- 1   can (14 ounces) sweetened condensed milk
- 1   package (14 ounces) flaked coconut
- 1   egg
- 1   teaspoon vanilla extract
- ½   teaspoon almond extract
- ½   cup all-purpose flour
- ¾   teaspoon baking powder
- ⅔   cup whole almonds

Preheat oven to 350 degrees. Melt chocolate chips and stir into sweetened condensed milk. In a large bowl, combine sweetened condensed milk mixture, coconut, egg, and extracts. In a small bowl, combine flour and baking powder. Add dry ingredients to coconut mixture; stir until well blended. Drop by teaspoonfuls onto an ungreased baking sheet. Press 1 almond into each cookie. Bake 8 to 10 minutes. Transfer cookies to a wire rack to cool. Store in an airtight container.
Yield: about 6½ dozen cookies

GARDEN TOTE

You will need green spray paint, 5" x 10" wooden tool tote, yellow acrylic paint,

paintbrush, wood-tone spray, three flower-seed packets, craft glue, several 22" lengths of natural raffia, hot glue gun, two 5½"h miniature garden tools, photocopy of tag design (page 151) on ecru card stock, colored pencils, and a black permanent fine-point marker.

Allow spray paint, paint, wood-tone spray, and craft glue to dry after each application.

1. Spray paint tote green. Paint handle of tote yellow. Paint a yellow border around front and sides of tote and stripes along edges of each side. Lightly apply wood-tone spray to tote.
2. Cut labels from flower seed packets. Arrange and use craft glue to glue labels on front of tote.
3. Tie raffia into a bow. Hot glue tools to tote; hot glue bow to handle of tools.
4. Cut out tag. Use colored pencils to color tag and marker to write message.

WELCOME, NEIGHBOR!

*E*xtend warm greetings to the new family on the block
with this folk-style pan filled with tangy Orange Sweet Rolls.
You'll be voted best neighbor, hands down!

ORANGE SWEET ROLLS

DOUGH
- 1   package (18¼ ounces) orange cake mix
- 4   to 4½ cups all-purpose flour
- 2   packages dry yeast
- 2½ cups very warm water (120 to 130 degrees)
- Vegetable oil cooking spray

FILLING
- ½   cup butter or margarine, softened
- 1   cup sugar
- 2   tablespoons grated orange zest

TOPPING
- ½   cup butter or margarine
- ¼   cup light corn syrup
- ¼   cup sugar

ICING
- 2½ cups confectioners sugar
- 4   to 5 tablespoons orange juice

Lightly grease two 9 x 13-inch aluminum foil pans (with plastic lids); set aside. For dough, combine cake mix, 4 cups flour, and yeast in a large bowl. Add warm water; stir until a soft dough forms. Turn onto a lightly floured surface and knead about 5 minutes or until dough becomes smooth and elastic, using additional flour as necessary. Place in a large bowl sprayed with cooking spray, turning once to coat top of dough.

Cover and let rise in a warm place (80 to 85 degrees) 1 hour or until doubled in size.

For filling, combine butter, sugar, and orange zest in a small bowl until well blended. Turn dough onto a lightly floured surface and punch down. Divide dough in half. Roll out half of dough into a 9 x 15-inch rectangle. Spread half of filling on dough. Beginning at 1 long edge, tightly roll up dough jellyroll style. Pinch seam to seal. Cut roll into 1-inch slices. Place in one prepared pan with cut side down and sides touching. Repeat with remaining dough and filling. Cover and let rise in a warm place (80 to 85 degrees) 1 hour or until almost doubled in size.

Preheat oven to 375 degrees. For topping, combine butter, corn syrup, and sugar in a small saucepan. Stirring constantly, cook over medium heat until butter melts and sugar dissolves. Pour topping over rolls. Bake 20 to 25 minutes or until rolls are lightly browned. Cool in pan 10 minutes.

For icing, combine confectioners sugar and orange juice in a small bowl; stir until smooth. Drizzle icing over warm rolls; serve warm.
Yield: 2 pans of rolls, about 15 rolls in each pan

"WELCOME, NEIGHBOR" PAN

For each pan, you will need tracing paper; yellow, pink, and blue card stock; craft glue stick; hot glue gun; one 1" dia. yellow button; four ⅜" dia. red buttons; black permanent fine-point marker; and a 9" x 13" aluminum foil pan with plastic lid.

1. Trace patterns, page 144, onto tracing paper; cut out. Using patterns, cut hand from yellow card stock and heart from pink card stock. Cut a 7" x 10¼" background from blue card stock.
2. Use glue stick to glue hand to background; glue heart to hand. Hot glue yellow button to center of heart and one red button to each corner of background. Use marker to draw "stitches" on heart and hand and to write message on background.
3. Hot glue background to top of plastic lid.

PUCKER UP

*U*ncork the buttery flavor of white wine and blend it with a little fresh mint and lemon zest. Sterilize the wine bottle and reuse it to hold the minted wine. Then create your own label with mint leaves and handmade paper. Serve this refreshing drink at cocktail hour with mixed nuts or your favorite dip.

MINTED LEMON WINE

- 1 bottle (750ml) white wine
- 1 tablespoon chopped fresh mint
- 1 teaspoon freshly grated lemon zest

In a 2-quart container, combine wine, mint, and zest. Cover and refrigerate for 24 hours for flavors to blend. Strain wine; serve chilled.
Yield: about 3 cups wine

DECORATED BOTTLE

You will need fresh mint leaves, empty white wine bottle, spray adhesive, 3" x 4½" piece of vellum, 4½" x 6" piece of handmade paper, ⅛" hole punch, raffia, and a black permanent fine-point marker.

1. Press several fresh mint leaves between pages of a heavy book for several days. Soak labels off wine bottle. (We used bottle from wine in recipe.)
2. For label, apply spray adhesive to one side of vellum piece. Center vellum piece on one side of handmade paper piece. Referring to photo for placement, punch two holes, close together, through vellum and handmade paper piece.
3. Cut three 6" lengths of raffia. Working

from front of label, insert raffia ends into holes. Cross raffia lengths at back of label and push ends back through holes, bringing ends to front of label. Trim ends if necessary.
4. Carefully apply spray adhesive to backs of several pressed mint leaves. Position leaves on front of label as desired. Using permanent marker, write recipe name on front of label. Apply spray adhesive to back of label. Referring to photo, position label on front of bottle. Wrap lengths of raffia around neck of bottle and tie off. Fill bottle with wine and replace cork or add a new stopper. Give wine with instructions to serve chilled.

SALSA ITALIANO

*A*dd international flair to a summertime party with this zippy Italian-style appetizer. For a hostess gift, pack a jar of Tomato-Basil Salsa in a beribboned basket along with fresh mozzarella cheese and crackers.

TOMATO-BASIL SALSA

- 1 can (28 ounces) diced tomatoes, drained
- ½ cup chopped fresh basil leaves
- ¼ cup olive oil
- 2 tablespoons chopped onion
- 2 tablespoons freshly squeezed lemon juice
- 2 tablespoons sugar
- 1 tablespoon balsamic vinegar
- 2 cloves garlic, coarsely chopped
- ½ teaspoon salt
- ½ teaspoon ground black pepper
  Fresh mozzarella cheese and crackers to serve

Process tomatoes, basil, oil, onion, lemon juice, sugar, vinegar, garlic, salt, and pepper in a food processor until well blended. Serve at room temperature with cheese slices and crackers. Store in an airtight container in refrigerator.

Yield: about 2½ cups salsa

SALSA BASKET

You will need a half-pint jar with lid, decorative-edge craft scissors, kraft paper, rubber band, raffia, photocopy of tag design (page 150) on ecru card stock, colored pencils, glue stick, 2⅜" x 2½" piece of green card stock, black permanent fine-point marker, 18" of 1½"w wired ribbon, basket (we used a

6½" sq. wooden basket with grapevine handle), ecru shredded paper, and a sprig of fresh basil.

1. Remove lid from jar; fill jar with salsa. Replace lid on jar. Measure across widest part of lid; add 2". Use decorative-edge scissors to cut a square from kraft paper the determined measurement. Center square over lid; secure with rubber band. Measure around lid; add 5". Cut several

lengths of raffia the determined measurement. Knot raffia around lid, covering rubber band.

2. Cut out tag. Use colored pencils to color tag. Glue tag to green card stock; glue card stock to kraft paper. Leaving a ¼" kraft paper border, cut out tag. Use marker to write message on tag.

3. Tie ribbon into a bow around handle of basket. Line basket with shredded paper. Place gifts in basket. Tuck in sprig of basil.

DIP AND DAISIES

Tucked in a handy basket along with toasted pita bread or tortilla chips, these protein-packed appetizers make great take-along fare for any occasion.

WHITE AND BLACK BEAN DIPS

WHITE BEAN DIP

1	can (15.8 ounces) great Northern beans, drained and rinsed
1	can (4½ ounces) chopped green chiles, drained
½	cup sour cream
¼	cup thick and chunky salsa
¼	cup chopped fresh cilantro
2	cloves garlic, minced
2	tablespoons freshly squeezed lime juice
1	teaspoon ground cumin
½	teaspoon ground white pepper
¼	teaspoon salt
	Tortilla chips or toasted pita bread to serve

For each bean dip, process beans, green chiles, sour cream, salsa, cilantro, garlic, lime juice, cumin, white pepper, and salt in a food processor just until blended. Store in an airtight container in refrigerator. Serve at room temperature with tortilla chips or toasted pita bread. *Yield:* about 2 cups bean dip

For black bean dip, substitute 1 can (15 ounces) black beans for great Northern beans.

DAISY BASKET AND BAG

You will need white spray paint, basket with wooden handles and feet (we used a 7" x 15" basket), black and white acrylic paint, paintbrush, ⅞"w black-and-white gingham silk ribbon, hot glue gun, 1⅓ yds. of 1⅜"w black-and-white gingham wired ribbon, 6" of floral wire, four 1" dia. artificial daisy flowers, white paper bag, decorative-edge craft scissors, hole punch, 12" of ⅜"w black-and-white grosgrain ribbon, one artificial daisy pick, excelsior, glass container, cellophane, and 4" of ⅛"w black satin ribbon.

Allow paint to dry after each application.

1. Spray paint basket white. Paint wooden part of handles and feet black. Use end of paintbrush to paint white dots on handles.
2. Measure around basket under rim; add ½". Cut a length from silk ribbon the determined measurement. Overlapping in front, glue silk ribbon around basket under rim. Use wired ribbon and follow *Making a Bow,* page 153, to make a bow with six 5" loops, 2" center loop, and two 4" streamers. Glue bow at center front of basket. Evenly space and glue daisy flowers along ribbon on front of basket.
3. Fill bag with chips. Trim top of bag with decorative-edge scissors. Fold top of bag 1½" to front. Punch two holes 1" apart in center folded portion of bag. Thread grosgrain ribbon through holes and knot at front of bag. Insert stem of pick under knot.
4. Line basket with excelsior. Place bag in basket. Fill glass container with dip; wrap in cellophane and tie with satin ribbon. Place gift in basket.

GARDEN BOUNTY

I f your summer garden overfloweth, never fear! Add zip to an ordinary day with an offering of rich White Chocolate Zucchini Bread. Appliqué a canvas tote bag with a medley of colorful vegetables to present your bountiful token.

WHITE CHOCOLATE-ZUCCHINI BREAD

¾ cup butter or margarine, softened
1¾ cups sugar
3 eggs
2 teaspoons vanilla extract
2 cups all-purpose flour
½ teaspoon baking powder
½ teaspoon baking soda
½ teaspoon salt
2 cups shredded unpeeled zucchini
¾ cup chopped pecans, toasted
3 ounces white baking chocolate, coarsely chopped

Preheat oven to 350 degrees. Line two 4½ x 8½-inch loaf pans with waxed paper; grease waxed paper. In a large bowl, cream butter and sugar until fluffy. Add eggs and vanilla; beat until smooth. In a small bowl, combine flour, baking powder, baking soda, and salt. Add dry ingredients to creamed mixture; stir until well blended. Stir in zucchini, pecans, and chocolate. Spoon into prepared pans. Bake 55 to 60 minutes or until a toothpick inserted in center of bread comes out clean. Cool in pans 5 minutes. Remove from pans and cool completely on a wire rack. Store in an airtight container.
Yield: 2 loaves bread

APPLIQUÉD VEGGIE BAGS

Refer to Making Appliqués, page 153, before beginning project.

For each bag, you will need paper-backed fusible web, fabrics for appliqués, bag (we used a 13¾" x 5¾" x 4" bag with handles), black permanent fine-point marker, several 15" lengths of natural and green raffia, hot glue gun, decorative-edge craft scissors, photocopy of tag design (page 151) on ecru card stock, hole punch, colored pencils, brown shredded paper, and plastic wrap.

1. Using patterns, page 143, and referring to *Making Appliqués,* page 153, make one eggplant and two each of onion, squash, tomato, tomato stem, carrot, and carrot top appliqués from fabrics.
2. Arrange and fuse appliqués on bag. Use marker to draw vines and dots on bag.
3. Set aside one length of raffia. Tie remaining raffia into a bow; glue bow to bag.
4. Using decorative-edge scissors and leaving a ⅛" border around design, cut out tag. Punch hole in top of tag. Use colored pencils to color tag. Use marker to write message on tag. Using raffia set aside in Step 3, attach tag to bow.
5. Fill bag with shredded paper. Wrap gift in plastic wrap. Place gift in bag.

FRUITY TWIST

Combine fruity flavors to create tempting Easy Strawberry-Orange Marmalade. Present a jar in a decorative berry bag for a simple-to-make gift your friends will enjoy.

EASY STRAWBERRY-ORANGE MARMALADE

2 packages (10 ounces each) sweetened frozen sliced strawberries, thawed
1 jar (12 ounces) orange marmalade
2 tablespoons freshly squeezed lemon juice
1 package (1¾ ounces) powdered fruit pectin
1 cup sugar

In a heavy large saucepan, combine strawberries with juice, marmalade, lemon juice, and pectin over medium-high heat. Bring to a rolling boil. Add sugar. Stirring constantly, bring to a rolling boil again and boil 1 minute. Remove from heat; skim off foam. Spoon marmalade into heat-resistant jars; cover and cool to room temperature. Store in refrigerator.
Yield: about 5 cups marmalade

STRAWBERRY BAGS

For each bag, you will need a 7" x 14" piece of red fabric, 3" x 14" piece of green fabric, pinking shears, half-pint jar with lid, and 14" of 4"w green paper twist.

1. Match right sides and one long edge of red and green fabrics; stitch ¼" from edge

to secure. Matching right sides and short edges, fold stitched fabric in half (fold of fabric is one side of bag). Stitch bottom and remaining side together ¼" from edges. Turn bag right side out. Trim top of bag with pinking shears.
2. Place gift in jar; place jar in bag. Knot paper twist around top of bag. Untwist ends of paper twist; trim ends to resemble leaves.

FIERY SUMMER SURPRISE

*T*hrow some hot dogs on the grill and get ready to enjoy the lazy days of summer! Our Fiery Tex-Mex Pepper Relish tastes awesome as a topping for grilled foods—and it's a dandy dip with chips. A papier-mâché egg becomes a cute watermelon gift box when you sponge paint the outside in cool shades of green.

FIERY TEX-MEX PEPPER RELISH

1 can (15¼ ounces) whole kernel corn, drained
1 can (14½ ounces) diced tomatoes, drained
1 jar (12 ounces) pickled jalapeño pepper slices, drained and chopped
1 cup chopped onion
½ cup chopped fresh cilantro
2 cloves garlic, minced

In a large bowl, combine corn, tomatoes, jalapeño pepper, onion, cilantro, and garlic; stir until well blended. Store in an airtight container in refrigerator.
Yield: about 4 cups relish

PAINTED WATERMELON EGG

You will need a 12" long papier-mâché egg box; green, yellow, red, black, and light green acrylic paint; paintbrush; 1"w piece of household sponge; and 1⅓ yds. of 1"w grosgrain ribbon.

Allow paint to dry after each application.

1. Separate egg halves. Paint outside of each half green.
2. Paint a 1"w yellow "rind" along edges of each rim on inside of egg. Paint remaining inside portion of each half red; paint black seeds on red areas.
3. Refer to *Sponge Painting,* page 154, to sponge paint light green stripes on outside of each egg half.
4. Place gift in egg; reassemble egg. Tie ribbon into a bow around egg.

CHOCOLATE EXPLOSION

S et off your own fireworks by giving Brownie Cupcakes for the Fourth of July. Recipients will never again be satisfied with plain cupcakes after trying these decadent little treats.

BROWNIE CUPCAKES

- ¾ cup butter or margarine
- 2 (1-ounce) squares semisweet chocolate
- 1 (1-ounce) square unsweetened chocolate
- 1¾ cups sugar
- 4 large eggs
- 1 teaspoon vanilla extract
- 1 cup all-purpose flour
- 2 tablespoons cocoa
- ⅛ teaspoon salt
- 1 cup chopped pecans

Preheat oven to 350 degrees. Melt butter and chocolate squares over low heat in a large heavy saucepan, stirring constantly. Remove from heat; stir in sugar. Add eggs, one at a time, whisking after each addition; stir in vanilla. Combine flour, cocoa, and salt; add to chocolate mixture, stirring until smooth. Stir in pecans. Spoon into muffin pans lined with paper baking cups, filling three-fourths full. Bake for 30 to 35 minutes.
Yield: 16 cupcakes

PATRIOTIC BASKET

You will need a red or natural-colored market basket, red spray paint (optional), pop-up craft sponge, white acrylic paint, paper plate, blue tissue paper, 1 yd. of 1"w blue grosgrain ribbon, and 1 yd. of ¼"w white grosgrain ribbon.

Allow paint to dry after each application.

1. If basket is red, skip this step. If basket is natural color, spray paint basket inside and out with red.
2. Trace star pattern, page 140, onto scrap of paper; cut out. Transfer star pattern to pop-up craft sponge; cut out. Wet sponge in water to expand and squeeze out excess water. Pour small puddle of white paint onto paper plate. Dip sponge in paint and sponge-paint stars on sides of basket as desired. (*Note:* If red paint bleeds through white stars, allow white paint to dry and then sponge-paint on top of stars a second time.)
3. Line basket with blue tissue paper. Place cupcakes in basket. Cut blue ribbon and white ribbon in half. Center one length of white ribbon along one length of blue ribbon. Holding both ribbons as one, tie ribbons into a bow around base of basket handle on one side of basket. Repeat with remaining ribbon lengths to tie bow around opposite side of basket handle.

FALL FOR BREAD

*C*ool *fall evenings just aren't complete without homemade bread.*
This loaf is best served warm and is a perfect companion to soup or stew.
Transport and serve the bread in this leafy bread basket. Both the basket
and the bread cloth are entirely no-sew.

CHEESY PEPPER BREAD

- 1 package (8 ounces) cream cheese, softened
- 2 tablespoons butter or margarine softened
- 2 eggs
- ½ cup milk
- 1½ cups shredded Monterey Jack cheese with jalapeño peppers
- 1 jar (2 ounces) chopped pimiento, drained
- 1 tablespoon chopped green onion
- 2 cups all-purpose flour
- 2 teaspoons baking powder
- ¼ teaspoon salt
- ⅛ teaspoon ground black pepper

Preheat oven to 350 degrees. In a medium bowl, combine cream cheese and butter; beat until fluffy. Add eggs and milk; beat until well blended. Beat in cheese, pimiento, and onion. In a large bowl, combine flour, baking powder, salt, and pepper. Add cream cheese mixture; stir just until blended. Spoon into a greased 5 x 9-inch loaf pan. Bake 50 to 55 minutes or until golden brown. Cool in pan 5 minutes. Transfer to a wire rack, remove from the pan, and cool completely. Store in an airtight container. Serve warm or toasted.

Yield: 1 loaf

BREAD BASKET AND CLOTH

You will need paper-backed fusible web scraps, fabric scraps in three different autumn colors, cotton batting scraps, ⅛" hole punch, raffia, purchased basket with handle, hot glue gun, ivory cotton dish towel or napkin, and plastic wrap.

1. *For basket,* press fusible web scraps onto wrong side of fabric scraps. Remove paper backing. Cut fabric scraps and batting scraps each into approximately 4" squares. Sandwich one batting scrap between two matching fabric scraps and fuse. Repeat with remaining fabric and batting scraps.

2. Trace desired number of acorns, acorn caps, and leaves in desired shapes, pages 144 and 145, onto fused fabric squares. Cut out shapes along pattern lines.

3. Punch two holes approximately ¼" apart in top of each leaf. Lace leaves onto one length of raffia. Add more raffia lengths to laced leaf length. Referring to photo and holding all raffia lengths as one, tie raffia around basket rim. If necessary, glue raffia in place on basket. Then glue acorns to handle of basket.

4. *For cloth,* press fusible web scraps onto wrong sides of fabric scraps. Trace one leaf A, two acorns, and two acorn caps, page 144, onto paper side of fabric scraps. (Acorn caps and bodies should be cut from different fabrics.) Cut out shapes along pattern lines. Remove paper backing. Referring to photo, fuse shapes on one corner of dish towel. To launder, wash by hand.

5. Place cloth in basket. Wrap gift in plastic wrap. Place gift in basket.

CAN'T WAIT FOR CORNBREAD

Cooking cornbread like waffles doubles the crusty edges so loved in this Southern staple. Combine a few simple ingredients to create a great dry mix and package the mix in an oven mitt. Your friends will be running to heat up their waffle irons.

WAFFLE IRON CORNBREAD

1	cup yellow cornmeal
½	cup all-purpose flour
2	tablespoons sugar
1	teaspoon baking powder
½	teaspoon baking soda
½	teaspoon salt
¼	teaspoon paprika
1½	cups buttermilk
3	tablespoons melted butter
1	egg, slightly beaten

In a large bowl, combine cornmeal, flour, sugar, baking powder, baking soda, salt, and paprika. In a small bowl combine buttermilk, melted butter, and egg. Add buttermilk mixture to dry ingredients, stirring just until blended. Bake in a hot waffle iron, using ½ to ¾ cup batter to each waffle. Serve warm.
Yield: 16 (4-inch) waffles

OVEN MITT PACKAGING

You will need a purchased oven mitt, 12" x 13" piece of coordinating fabric, thread to match fabric, zip-top plastic bag, jute twine, 12" of 1½"w sheer ribbon, ⅝"w woven ribbon, raffia, wooden spoon, coordinating recipe card, and a hole punch.

1. To make fabric bag, fold fabric in half, matching right sides, so that fabric measures 6" x 13". Using ½" seam allowance, sew along bottom and side of fabric. Turn bag right side out. Fill zip-top plastic bag with cornbread mix (first seven ingredients) and seal. Insert plastic bag in fabric bag. Fold approximately 2½" of top raw edge of bag to inside. Tie jute twine into a bow around top of bag. Insert filled fabric bag in oven mitt.
2. Tie both ribbons and several lengths of raffia into a bow around handle of wooden spoon. Slip wooden spoon inside oven mitt next to filled fabric bag.
3. Write instructions for making cornbread on recipe card. Punch hole in top corner of recipe card. Use length of raffia to tie recipe card to oven mitt.

RISE AND SHINE!

*T*empt a sleepyhead out of bed with our Cinnamon Swirl Coffee Cake. Topped with a sweet glaze, the breakfast treat begins with a boxed cake mix. The cheery cake pan topper is fashioned using bristol board and dimensional paint.

CINNAMON SWIRL COFFEE CAKE

CAKE
- 1 package (18¼ ounces) white cake mix
- 4 eggs
- 1 container (8 ounces) sour cream
- 1½ cups sugar, divided
- ¾ cup butter or margarine, melted
- 1 cup golden raisins
- 1 tablespoon ground cinnamon

GLAZE
- 1 cup confectioners sugar
- ⅓ cup butter or margarine, melted
- 1 tablespoon milk

Preheat oven to 325 degrees. For cake, combine cake mix, eggs, sour cream, ½ cup sugar, and melted butter in a large bowl; beat until well blended. Pour batter into a greased 9 x 13-inch baking pan. In a small bowl, combine remaining 1 cup sugar, raisins, and cinnamon. Sprinkle over cake batter; swirl with a knife. Bake 42 to 47 minutes or until a toothpick inserted in center of cake comes out clean. Cool in pan 30 minutes. For glaze, combine confectioners sugar, melted butter, and milk in a small bowl; stir until smooth. Drizzle glaze over warm cake. Serve warm or cool completely. Store in an airtight container. *Yield:* about 15 servings

"RISE AND SHINE" CAKE PAN

You will need tracing paper; transfer paper; 7⅛" x 10⅞" piece of blue bristol board; white, yellow, red, blue, green, and black dimensional paint; ¾"w double-sided tape; 9" x 13" cake pan with lid; hot glue gun; four ⅝" dia. buttons; and ¾"w fabric ribbon.

1. Trace design, pages 146 and 147, onto tracing paper. Use transfer paper to transfer design to bristol board. Using dimensional paint and referring to design for color placement, hold tip of paint bottle just above bristol board and squeeze small dots of paint along lines of design. Allow to dry.
2. Use tape to attach bristol board to lid. Glue one button to each corner of board.
3. For ribbon trim, measure width and length of lid; add 8" to each measurement. Cut two lengths of ribbon for each measurement. Center one ribbon length along each edge of lid; use tape to secure. Knot ends together at corners; notch ribbon ends.

MUFFINS FROM THE HEART

*S*hare a little love with a friend—
drop off a batch of our Cherry-Berry
Muffin Mix. Simply pack the fruity
ingredients in a homespun "flour
sack" and tuck it into a heart-shaped
serving bowl along with instructions
for baking.

CHERRY-BERRY MUFFIN MIX

2 cups all-purpose flour
1 cup sugar
¼ cup buttermilk powder
1 teaspoon baking soda
½ teaspoon salt
½ cup chilled butter, cut into pieces
1 package (6 ounces) sweetened
    dried cherry and berry fruit mix,
    chopped (about 1¼ cups)
½ cup chopped walnuts, toasted
1 teaspoon grated lemon zest

In a medium bowl, combine flour, sugar,
buttermilk powder, baking soda, and salt.
Using a pastry blender or 2 knives, cut butter
into dry ingredients until mixture resembles
coarse meal. Stir in fruit, toasted walnuts,
and lemon zest.

Divide mix into 2 resealable plastic bags
(about 2¾ cups mix each). Store in
refrigerator. Give with baking instructions.
Yield: 2 bags mix, about 2¾ cups each

To bake: Store muffin mix in refrigerator
until ready to prepare. In a medium bowl,
combine 1 cup water and 1 bag muffin mix;
stir just until moistened. Fill paper-lined
muffin cups about two-thirds full. Bake in a
400-degree oven 18 to 20 minutes or until a
toothpick inserted in center of muffin comes
out clean and tops are golden. Serve warm.
Yield: about 9 muffins

MUFFIN GIFT SET

You will need matte spray sealer, heart-
shaped textured wooden bowl, red acrylic
paint, paintbrush, sandpaper, tack cloth,
fabric, pinking shears, paper-backed
fusible web, canvas bag (we used a
6½" x 11" canvas bag), zip-top plastic
bag, 12" of jute twine, 4" x 6" piece of ecru
card stock, hot glue gun, ¾" dia. button,
and a black permanent fine-point marker.

*Allow sealer and paint to dry after each
application.*

1. Apply sealer to bowl. Paint bowl red.
Lightly sand bowl; wipe bowl with tack
cloth. Apply an additional coat of sealer.
2. For liner, draw around rim of bowl twice
on wrong side of fabric. Cut out two fabric
hearts 3" outside drawn lines. Matching
wrong sides, sew hearts together ¾" from
edges. Trim edges with pinking shears.
3. Using pattern, page 142, and pinking
shears to cut out shape, follow *Making
Appliqués,* page 153, to make one heart
appliqué from fabric. Fuse heart to bag.
Fill zip-top plastic bag with muffin mix and
seal. Place gift in fabric bag. Knot twine at
top of bag.
4. For tag, matching short edges, fold card
stock in half. Use pinking shears to cut a
¾" x 12" strip from fabric. Tie strip into a
bow. Glue bow to tag; glue button to knot
of bow. Use marker to write message on
tag and baking instructions inside tag.

TOUCHDOWN FOR PIZZA DIP

*D*on't go to your next football party empty-handed. Take our Warm Pizza Dip, and you have an appetizer that will have fans cheering. For extra spirit, decorate the straw pie basket with the color of your host's favorite team.

WARM PIZZA DIP

 1 package (8 ounces) cream cheese, softened
 1 container (8 ounces) sour cream
 ½ teaspoon dried oregano leaves
 ¼ teaspoon garlic powder
 ¼ teaspoon salt
 ¼ teaspoon ground red pepper
 ½ cup purchased pizza sauce
 ½ cup chopped pepperoni slices (half of 3.5 ounce package)
 ¼ cup chopped green onions
 ¼ cup sliced ripe olives
 1 cup (4 ounces) shredded mozzarella cheese
   Tortilla chips to serve

In a medium bowl, beat cream cheese until fluffy. Add sour cream, oregano, garlic powder, salt, and red pepper; beat until smooth. Spread cream cheese mixture in bottom and up sides of an ungreased 9-inch pie plate. Layer pizza sauce over cream cheese mixture. Toss together pepperoni, green onions, olives, and mozzarella cheese; sprinkle over the top. Cover and store in refrigerator. Give with baking and serving instructions.
Yield: about 2¾ cups dip
To bake and serve: Bake, uncovered, in a 350-degree oven about 25 minutes or until heated through and cheese melts. Serve warm with tortilla chips.

SERVING TRAY

You will need 2" to 2½"w paper ribbon in two different colors for your favorite team, stapler, hot glue gun, 11" dia. straw pie basket, florist wire, plastic football party trinkets, large cellophane bag, tortilla chips, 16" of checked sheer ribbon, 2" x 4" piece of white paper, marker in color to match ribbon, hole punch, and a black writing pen.

1. Cut base ribbon color in 10" lengths; cut top ribbon color in 8" lengths. (You will need approximately 15 to 20 lengths of each color.) Fold each length in half and staple short ends together. Using scissors and beginning on folded end of ribbon lengths, fringe each folded ribbon length by cutting approximately ⅜"w slits.
2. Turn pie basket upside down. Glue stapled edge of fringed top ribbon color to bottom rim of pie basket. Glue stapled edge of fringed base ribbon color on top of top ribbon color, aligning stapled edges.
3. Cut 35" length of each color of paper ribbon. Cut each 35" length into ⅜"w strips. Make multiple loops with ribbons and then secure center of loops with florist wire. Glue looped bow to top rim of basket. Glue football trinkets to center of bow. Repeat to make a second bow with trinkets for opposite side of basket.
4. Place glass pie plate filled with gift in center of basket for serving. Fill large cellophane bag with tortilla chips. Tie top of bag with checked sheer ribbon.
5. For tag, fold white paper in half. Using colored marker, draw motif from team on front of tag. Punch hole in corner of tag. Use writing pen to write baking instructions inside tag. Thread tag onto sheer ribbon.

GOOD MORNING!

*A great start to the day means eating a good breakfast, and
Wheat Pancake Mix and Peanut Butter Syrup provide a yummy way to have a
healthy day! Our recipe makes enough for five families, so neighborhood gift-giving is a snap.
Simply tie bags of the mix with greenery and ribbon, fill jars with the golden syrup,
and present them in painted wooden trays filled with peanuts.*

WHEAT PANCAKE MIX AND PEANUT BUTTER SYRUP

PANCAKE MIX

3¾	cups all-purpose flour
3	cups whole-wheat flour
1¾	cups plus 2 tablespoons buttermilk powder
¾	cup sugar
1	tablespoon baking soda
1	tablespoon salt

SYRUP

2	bottles (16 ounces each) pancake syrup
1	cup smooth peanut butter

For pancake mix, combine flours, buttermilk powder, sugar, baking soda, and salt in a large bowl; stir until well blended. Divide mix into 5 resealable plastic bags (about 2 cups in each bag). Store in refrigerator. Give with serving instructions.

For syrup, combine pancake syrup and peanut butter in a medium bowl; stir well to blend. Divide syrup into five 8-ounce jars with lids. Give with pancake mix and serving instructions.

Yield: about 10 cups pancake mix and about 5 cups syrup

To serve: Grease and preheat griddle. Combine 1 bag pancake mix (about 2 cups), 1 cup water, 1 egg, and 2 tablespoons vegetable oil; stir just until moistened. Let stand 5 minutes. For each pancake, pour about ¼ cup batter onto griddle. Cook until top of pancake has a few bubbles and bottom is golden brown. Turn with a spatula and cook until remaining side is golden brown. Serve warm pancakes with peanut butter syrup.

Yield: about 9 pancakes

WOODEN TRAY AND BAG

You will need a wooden tray (we used a 8½" x 10" tray); green acrylic paint; paintbrush; sandpaper; tack cloth; 6" x 11" piece of fabric; zip-top plastic bag; 20" each of ¼"w grosgrain ribbon and ⅜"w satin ribbon; two 20" lengths of ⅝"w sheer ribbon; hot glue gun; artificial greenery pick; unshelled peanuts; and two napkins.

1. Paint tray green; allow to dry. Lightly sand tray to give a weathered appearance. Wipe tray with tack cloth.
2. For bag, press each short edge of fabric 3" to the wrong side; stitch to secure. Matching short edges and wrong sides, fold fabric in half. Stitch side seams ¼" from edges to secure. Turn bag right side out.
3. Fill zip-top plastic bag with pancake mix and seal bag. Place gift in fabric bag. Using one 20" length of each ribbon, knot ribbons around top of bag. Glue greenery to knot; glue two peanuts to greenery.
4. Fill tray with remaining peanuts. Nestle gift bag in peanuts. Cut remaining sheer ribbon in half. Tie up napkins, as shown in photo, using sheer ribbon, and place in tray.

PUMPKIN HARVEST

Pumpkin makes this biscotti a fall favorite. Served with tea or coffee, this crunchy treat brings warmth to a chilly November day. Leaf-etched plates make a fitting fall presentation.

PUMPKIN PIE BISCOTTI

3½ cups all-purpose flour
1½ cups firmly packed brown sugar
2 teaspoons baking powder
½ teaspoon salt
2 teaspoons pumpkin pie spice
½ cup canned, mashed pumpkin
2 large eggs, lightly beaten
1 tablespoon vanilla extract
2 tablespoons butter or margarine
1¼ cups macadamia nuts, coarsely
    chopped

Preheat oven to 350 degrees. Combine flour, brown sugar, baking powder, salt, and pumpkin pie spice in a large bowl; stir well. Combine pumpkin, eggs, and vanilla, stirring well with a wire whisk. Slowly add pumpkin mixture to flour mixture, stirring until dry ingredients are moistened. (Mixture will be very crumbly; it will gradually become moist after stirring.) Melt butter in a large skillet over medium heat; add macadamia nuts. Cook, stirring constantly, until nuts are browned. Remove from heat and cool completely. Knead or gently stir cooled nuts into dough.

Place dough on a lightly floured surface and divide into 4 portions. Lightly flour hands and shape each portion into a 1 x 15-inch log. Place logs 3 inches apart on lightly greased cookie sheets. Bake for 23 minutes; cool logs 15 minutes. Reduce oven temperature to 300 degrees. Cut each log diagonally into ½-inch slices, using a serrated knife. Place slices on ungreased cookie sheets. Bake for 15 minutes. Cool completely on wire racks.
Yield: about 8 dozen cookies

ETCHED PLATES

You will need peel-and-stick vinyl shelf covering; plain, clear glass dessert plates; rubber gloves; sponge paintbrush; etching cream; and 1 yd. of 1¼"w autumn colored ribbon.

Be sure to wear rubber gloves when working with etching cream to protect your hands.

1. Trace leaf patterns, page 149, onto scraps of paper. Transfer patterns to vinyl shelf covering and cut desired number and sizes. (Make separate leaves for each plate. We used 9 to 11 leaves on each plate.)
2. For each plate, turn plate over. Remove paper backing from vinyl shelf covering leaves; adhere leaves as desired to back of plate. Wearing rubber gloves and using sponge paintbrush, apply a thick coat of etching cream to back of plate. Allow etching cream to sit for five minutes. Still wearing rubber gloves, rinse plates under running water to remove cream. Remove peel-and-stick stencils. Wash plates by hand with soap and warm water.
3. For presenting plates, stack plates and tie up with ribbon.

This could be the easiest pie you ever made. Just mix and pour the ingredients in the pie shell. Give the pie surrounded by a bountiful fall wreath. Make sure to attach a backing to the wreath to hold the pie.

SPEEDY SWEET POTATO PIE

1 (16-ounce) can cut sweet
   potatoes, drained and mashed
1 (14-ounce) can sweetened
   condensed milk
1 teaspoon vanilla extract
½ teaspoon ground nutmeg
2 large eggs
1 unbaked 9-inch pastry shell

Preheat oven to 425 degrees. Beat sweet potatoes, condensed milk, vanilla, nutmeg, and eggs at medium speed of an electric mixer until well blended. Pour filling into pastry shell. Bake for 15 minutes. Reduce oven temperature to 350 degrees and bake 30 to 35 minutes longer or until a knife inserted in center comes out clean.
Yield: about 8 servings

WREATH PIE SERVER

You will need a 12" dia. straw wreath, 3 yds. of 1¼"w gold ribbon, hot glue gun, spray adhesive, 12" dia. cardboard circle, two 12" dia. circles of gift wrap in autumn colors, awl or similar sharp object, florist wire, silk autumn leaves, and artificial flowers and miniature gourds.

1. Wrap wreath with ribbon as shown in photo, securing ends with hot glue.

2. Spray one side of cardboard circle with spray adhesive. Place one circle of gift wrap faceup on sprayed side of cardboard circle; press in place. Repeat to cover opposite side of cardboard circle with remaining gift wrap circle.
3. Using awl or similar sharp object, punch four pairs of holes in cardboard circle, evenly spacing pairs of holes around circle and making them approximately 1" to 1½" in from outside edge. Cut four 12" lengths of florist wire.

Working from bottom of cardboard circle, insert one wire length into each pair of holes so that free ends of wire are on top of circle. Center ribbon-wrapped wreath over cardboard circle. Twist wire ends around wreath to attach it to cardboard circle, concealing wires beneath ribbon.
4. Using additional pieces of florist wire, attach silk leaves and artificial flowers and gourds to top of wreath as shown in photo. Place gift in wreath for serving.

CORNY CANDY ON A STICK

*C*hock-full of popcorn, teddy
bear crackers, and candy corn, this
candy is a must for kids of all ages
on Halloween. Gather your children
to help shape the balls, as you need
to work quickly. Wrap the candy in
plastic first to prevent balls from
sticking to the tissue paper.

CORNY CANDY ON A STICK

- 50 large marshmallows
- ⅓ cup butter or margarine, cut up
- 20 cups freshly popped popcorn
- 2 cups teddy bear-shaped chocolate graham cracker cookies
- 2½ cups candy corn
  Vegetable oil cooking spray
- 20 wooden craft sticks

Combine marshmallows and butter in a
large Dutch oven. Cook over medium-low
heat until marshmallows melt, stirring
occasionally. Remove mixture from heat.
Combine popped corn and graham
cracker cookies in a large bowl. Pour
marshmallow mixture over popped corn
mixture, tossing to coat. Add candy corn;
stir well. Coat hands with cooking spray,
and shape popped popcorn mixture into
3-inch balls, pressing together firmly.
Insert a wooden craft stick in each
popcorn ball. Let cool on waxed paper.
Wrap balls in plastic wrap and then in
tissue paper or cellophane.
Yield: about 20 (3-inch) popcorn balls

JACK-O'-LANTERN PACKAGING

You will need clear plastic wrap, green
permanent marker, orange tissue paper or

cellophane, raffia, black Fun Foam, and
thick craft glue.

1. Wrap each serving in clear plastic wrap.
Leaving approximately ½" to 1" of stick at
base of each treat uncolored, color both
sides of remaining area of stick with green
marker.
2. For each serving, cut an approximately
12" square of orange tissue paper or

cellophane. Place plastic-wrapped treat in
center of tissue paper square. Gather
tissue paper around treat and tie at top,
near base of stick, with several lengths of
raffia. Trim raffia if necessary.
3. Transfer jack-o'-lantern face pattern,
page 140, onto scrap of paper; cut out.
Transfer one face for each treat onto black
Fun Foam; cut out. Glue face to front of
tissue-wrapped treat; allow to dry.

*C*andy sprinkles and a spiderweb design dress up these chocolaty peanut butter cakes. A sponge-painted window box makes a haunting presentation.

CHOCOLATE-PEANUT BUTTER RICE CAKES

  24 ounces chocolate candy coating, chopped
1¼ cups semisweet chocolate chips
   1 package (7.33 ounces) peanut butter-flavored rice cakes
  ⅓ cup peanut butter chips
   1 teaspoon vegetable shortening
     Brown and orange sprinkles

In top of a double boiler, melt candy coating and chocolate chips over hot, not simmering, water. Remove from heat (if chocolate begins to harden, return to heat). Spoon chocolate over tops and sides of 7 rice cakes. Place on lightly greased waxed paper. Place peanut butter chips and shortening in a small heavy-duty resealable plastic bag. Microwave on medium power (50%) 2½ minutes or until chips melt, squeezing bag after each minute. Snip off 1 corner of bag to create a small opening. Beginning at center of each cake, pipe 4 circles about ¼ inch apart onto wet chocolate. Beginning at smallest circle, pull a toothpick through circles to outer edge to make spiderweb design. Spoon chocolate over remaining rice cakes and cover with sprinkles. Allow chocolate to harden. Store in an airtight container in a cool place.
Yield: about 14 rice cakes

HALLOWEEN GIFT BOX

You will need tracing paper; 9½" x 14½" shirt box with lid; craft knife; cutting mat; compressed craft sponges; orange, black, and green acrylic paint; paintbrush; black permanent medium-point marker; craft glue; and a 9" x 13" piece of clear cellophane.

Allow paint to dry after each application.

1. Using patterns, page 145, follow *Making Patterns,* page 152, to make pumpkin and cat; cut out. Draw around pumpkin pattern on center of box lid. Use craft knife to cut out opening along drawn line.
2. Refer to *Sponge Painting,* page 154, to sponge paint top and sides of lid orange. Draw around cat pattern on sponge; cut out. Sponge paint black cats on lid. Paint green stem over pumpkin opening.
3. Use marker to draw vine, to outline stem, and to draw "stitches" around pumpkin.
4. Apply glue to inside of box lid around opening. Smooth cellophane over opening; allow to dry. Fill box with gift.

GIVE THANKS FOR PECAN TARTS

*Y*ou *don't have to make an entire pecan pie to enjoy that rich buttery flavor.*
Easy Pecan Tarts are baked in premade tart shells, but no one will ever know.
These one-serving tarts are a perfect gift for a special friend.
Just place each in a small box decorated for fall.

EASY PECAN TARTS

2   large eggs, lightly beaten
1   cup chopped pecans
¾   cup firmly packed brown sugar
2   tablespoons butter or margarine, melted
1   teaspoon vanilla extract
    Pinch of salt
8   (2-inch) unbaked tart shells
    Garnishes: whipped cream, pecan halves

Preheat oven to 425 degrees. Combine eggs, pecans, brown sugar, butter, vanilla, and salt. Spoon pecan mixture into tart shells. Place filled shells on a baking sheet. Bake for 16 to 18 minutes or until filling is set. Cool completely on a wire rack. Garnish, if desired.
Yield: 8 tarts

AUTUMN BOXES

For each box, you will need a 4" sq. papier-mâché box, tape measure, decorative paper, spray adhesive, corrugated cardboard in desired colors, decorative-edge craft scissors (optional), awl or similar sharp object, raffia, silk autumn leaves, dried florals (optional), and tissue paper.

1. Remove lid from box. Measure depth of box bottom; also measure distance around box bottom and add 1". Cut rectangular piece of decorative paper equal to these measurements. Spray sides of box bottom with spray adhesive. With long edges of decorative paper aligned with top and bottom edges of box bottom, wrap decorative paper around sides of box. Measure top of box lid. Cut piece of decorative paper equal to this measurement. Apply spray adhesive to top of box lid. Adhere decorative paper to top of box lid.
2. Measure depth of rim of box lid and add ¼"; also measure distance around box lid. Cut rectangular strip of corrugated cardboard equal to these measurements. If desired, use regular scissors or decorative-edge scissors to add scallops to one long edge of corrugated cardboard strip. Apply spray adhesive to rim of box lid. With straight edge of corrugated cardboard strip flush with top edge of box lid, adhere corrugated cardboard strip to rim of box lid. If desired, cut strips of corrugated cardboard to adhere across lid top or down sides of box bottom. Or if desired, cut a square of corrugated cardboard equal to size of lid top and adhere to lid.
3. Using awl or similar sharp object, punch two holes close together in center of box lid. Working from under lid and holding several lengths of raffia as one, push ends of raffia through these holes and bring to top of lid. Gather small bunch of silk leaves and, if desired, dried florals. Tie leaves and dried florals to top of lid using raffia.
4. Line box bottom with tissue paper and place one gift in box.

PATTERNS

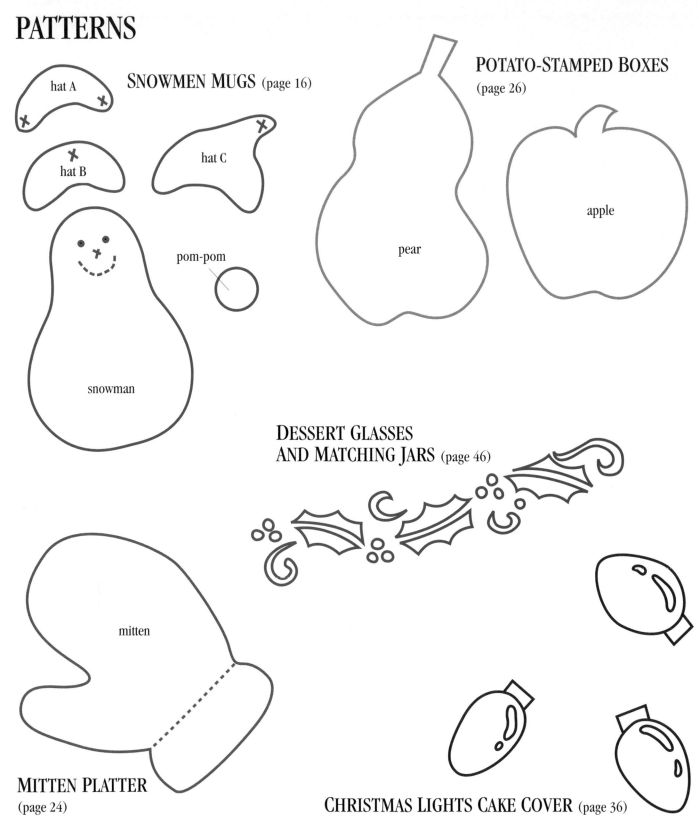

SNOWMEN MUGS (page 16)

hat A

hat B

hat C

pom-pom

snowman

POTATO-STAMPED BOXES (page 26)

pear

apple

DESSERT GLASSES
AND MATCHING JARS (page 46)

MITTEN PLATTER
(page 24)

mitten

CHRISTMAS LIGHTS CAKE COVER (page 36)

X	DMC	B'ST	ANC.	COLOR
•	blanc		2	white
■	310	⁄	403	black
✓	350		11	coral
☒	415		398	lt grey
⊖	435		1046	tan
◆	436		1045	lt tan
Π	676		891	lt gold
♥	699		923	dk green
◉	702		226	green
□	704		256	lt green
○	725		305	topaz
+	813		161	lt blue
▬	817	⁄	13	dk coral
♡	945		881	flesh
✳	3326		36	pink
●	310		403	black Fr. Knot

CROSS-STITCHED SANTA BAG

(page 15)

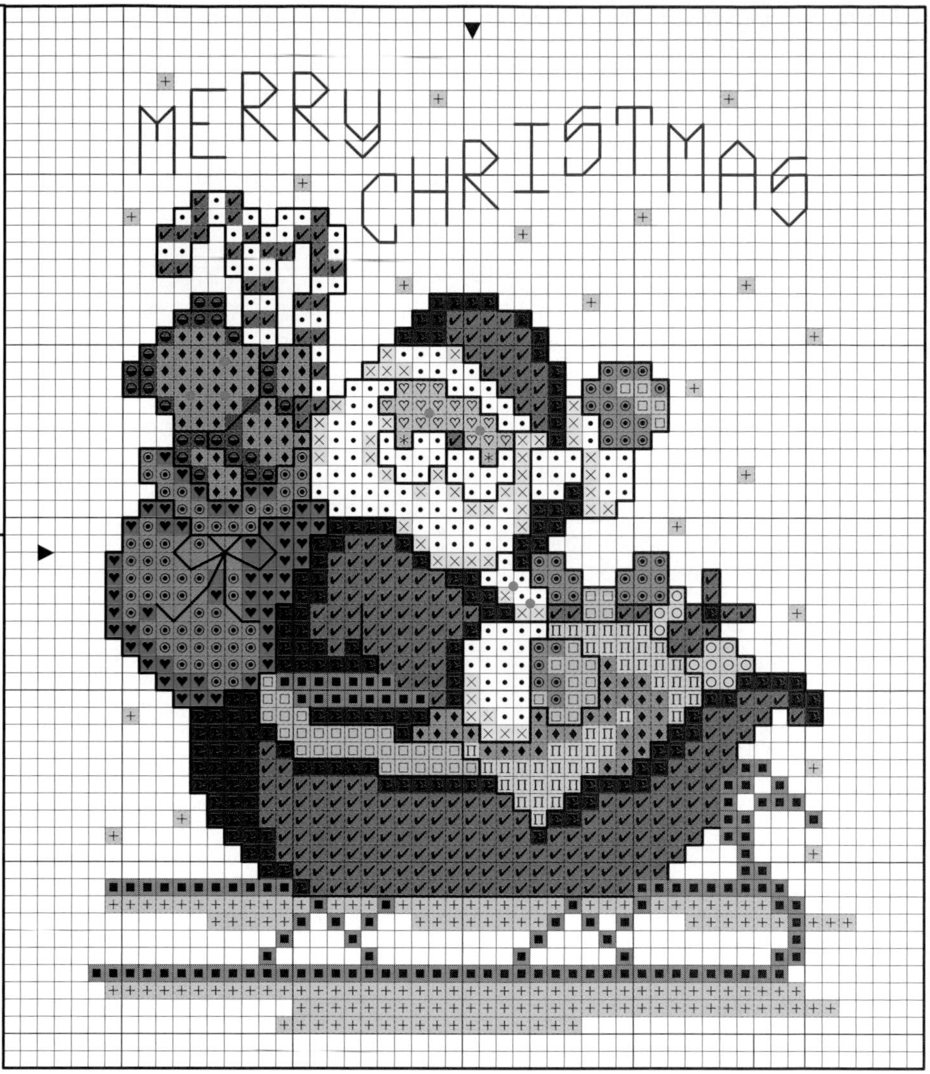

ANGEL ORNAMENT BASKET (page 84)

X	DMC	¼X	B'ST	COLOR
⁙	blanc			White
+	353			Rose
	356		⁄	Terra Cotta, Med
✳	434	◿		Brown, Lt
★	436			Tan
▽	754	◿		Peach Flesh, Lt
⁙	760			Salmon
	898		⁄	Coffee Brown , Vy Lt
	931	◿		Antique Blue
⊙	948	◿		Peach Flesh, Vy Lt
V	3072			Beaver Grey , Vy Lt
	3328		⁄	Salmon Med

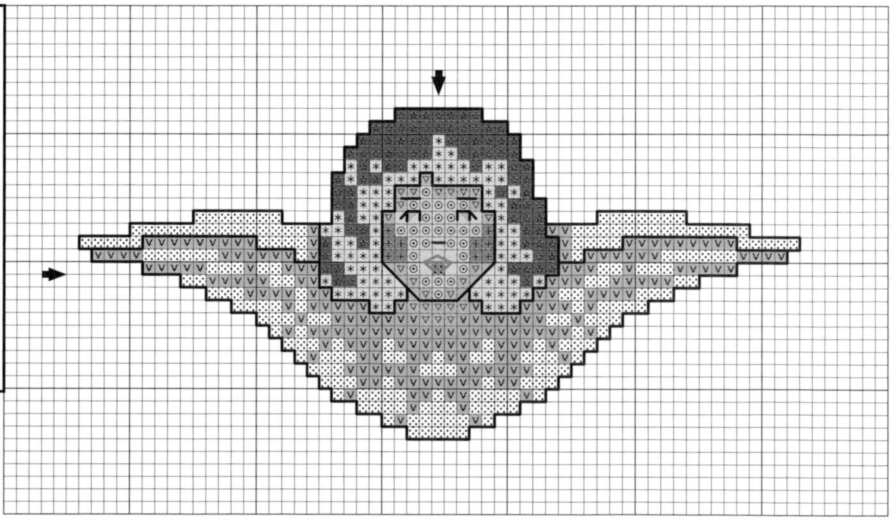

PATTERNS
(continued)

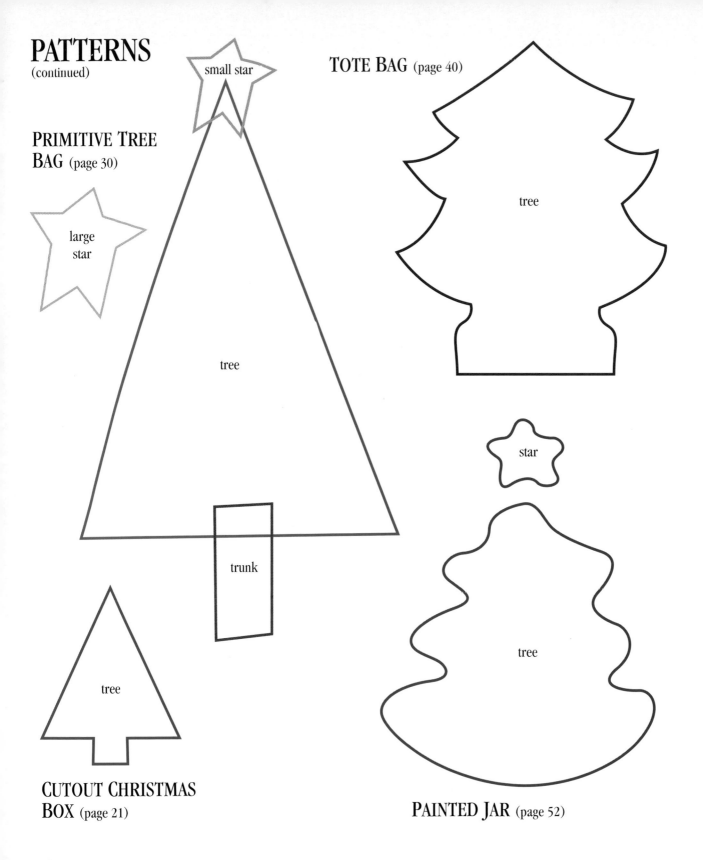

PRIMITIVE TREE BAG (page 30)

small star

large star

tree

trunk

TOTE BAG (page 40)

tree

star

tree

CUTOUT CHRISTMAS BOX (page 21)

tree

PAINTED JAR (page 52)

BUBBLE WRAP SANTA BAG

(page 32)

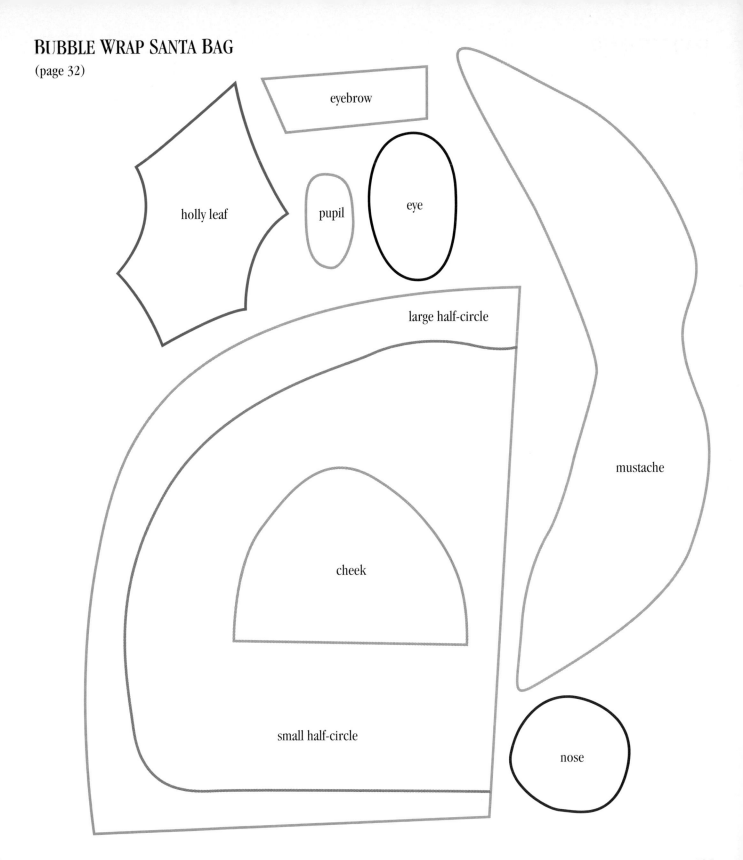

eyebrow

holly leaf

pupil

eye

large half-circle

mustache

cheek

small half-circle

nose

PATTERNS (continued)

GINGERBREAD MAN DISH TOWEL
(page 38)

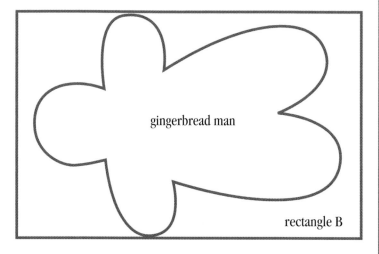

gingerbread man

rectangle B

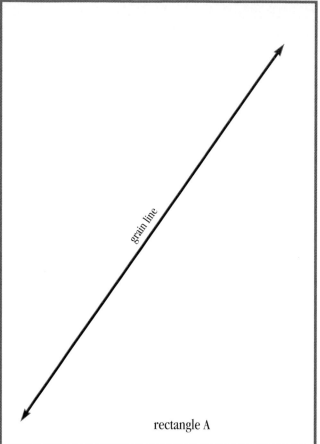

grain line

rectangle A

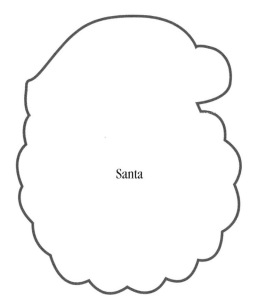

Santa

SANTA LOLLIPOP COOKIES
(page 43)

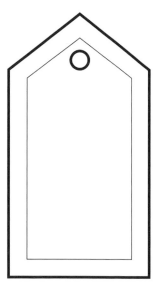

"HO HO HO" TAG
(page 43)

shamrock

SHAMROCK TAGS (page 97)

NAPKIN RINGS
AND MATCHING
CANISTER
(page 70)

star

tree

small star

large star

STAR-STAMPED PIE BOX
(page 68)

PEPPERMINT JARS (page 44)

PATTERNS (continued)

REINDEER BASKET
(page 50)

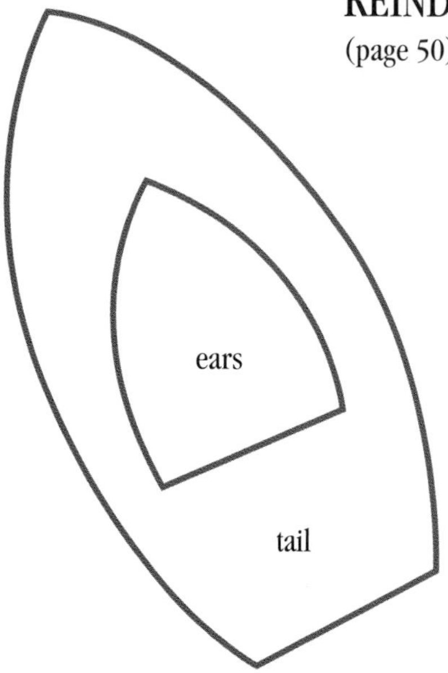

ears

tail

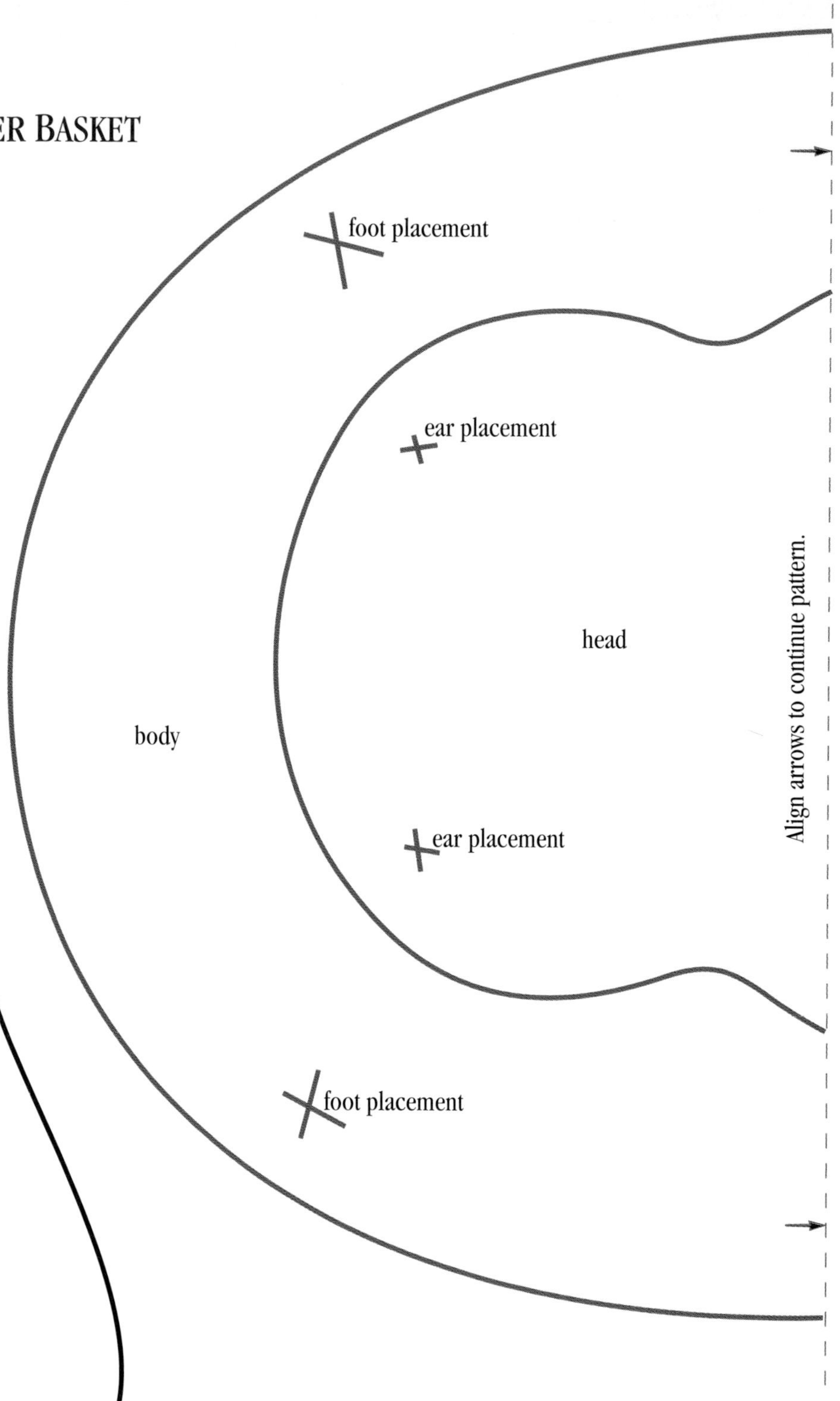

foot placement

ear placement

body

head

ear placement

foot placement

Align arrows to continue pattern.

ANGEL BASKET
(page 88)

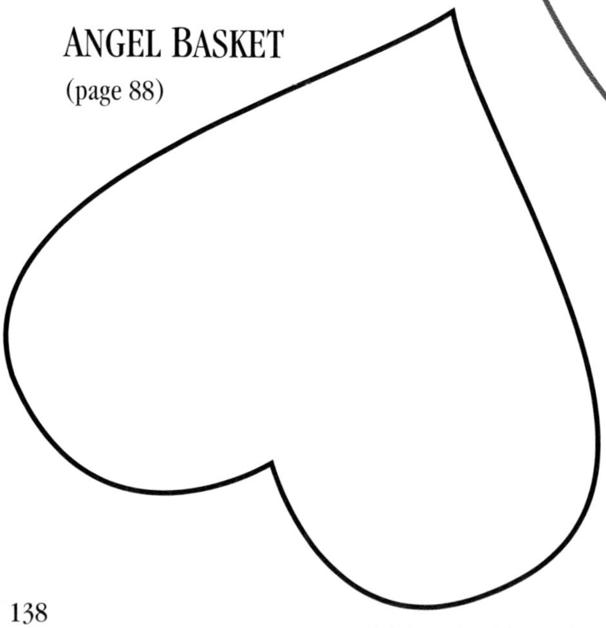

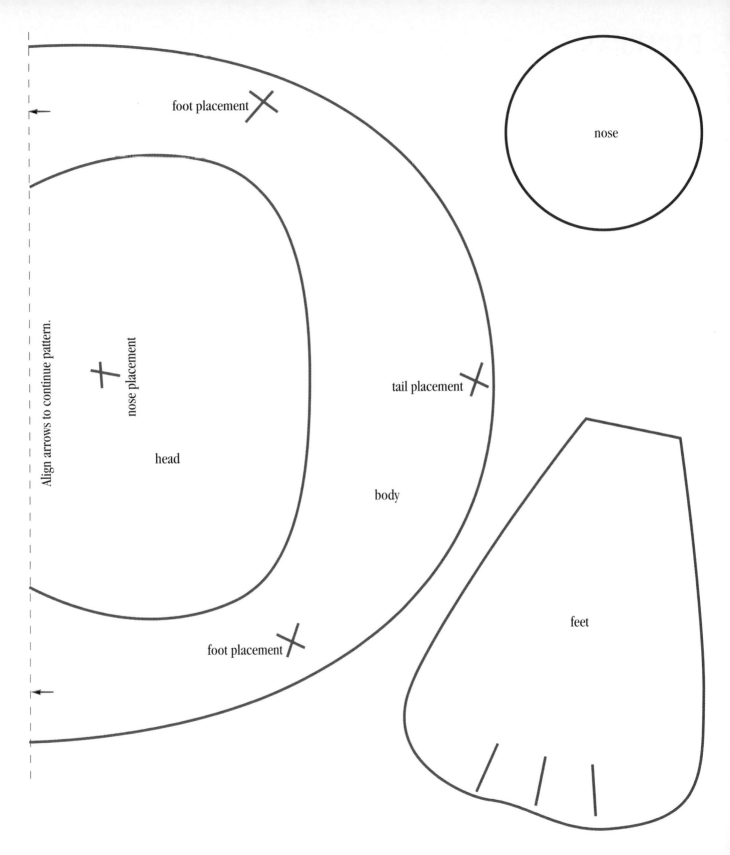

foot placement

nose

Align arrows to continue pattern.

nose placement

head

tail placement

body

foot placement

feet

139

PATTERNS (continued)

PAPER STOCKING (page 53)

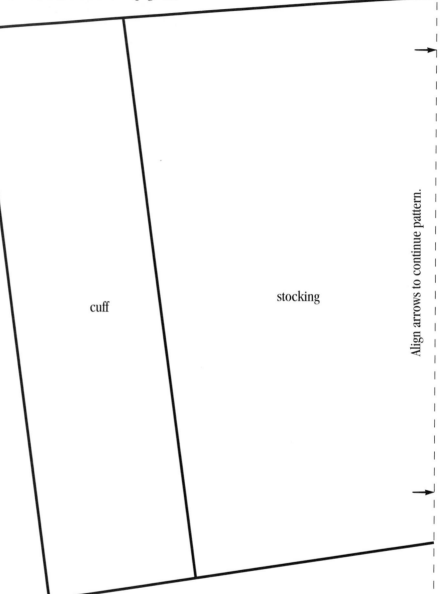

background

large heart

small heart

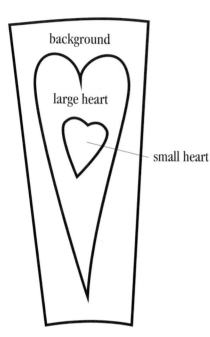

cuff

stocking

Align arrows to continue pattern.

APPLIQUÉD FLOWERPOT
(page 48)

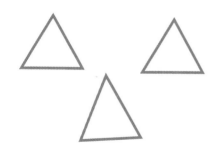

JACK-O'-LANTERN PACKAGING
(page 128)

PATRIOTIC BASKET
(page 117)

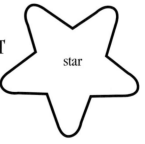

star

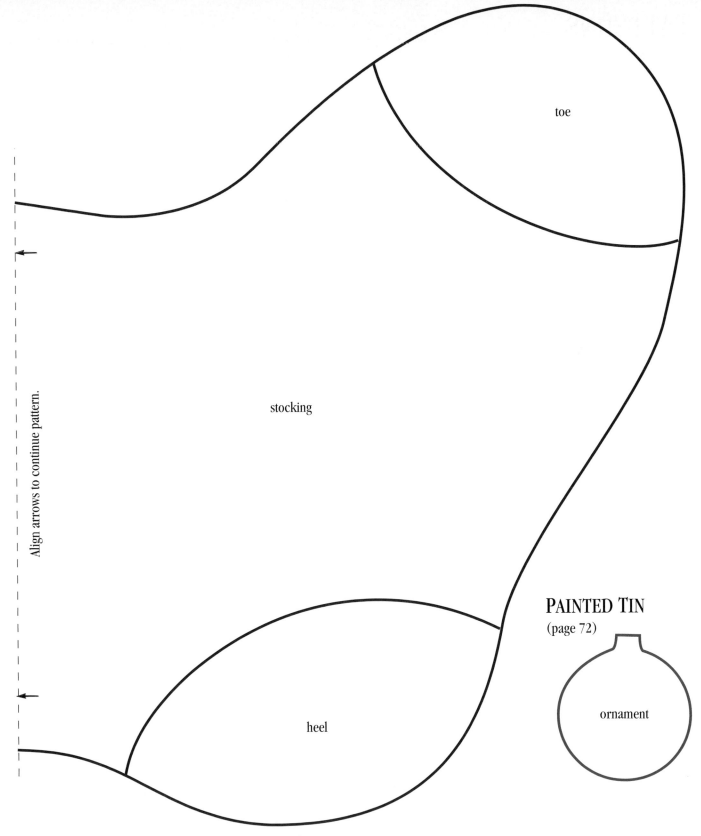

toe

Align arrows to continue pattern.

stocking

PAINTED TIN
(page 72)

heel

ornament

PATTERNS
(continued)

JESTER HATS
(page 41)

tab

Align arrows to continue pattern.

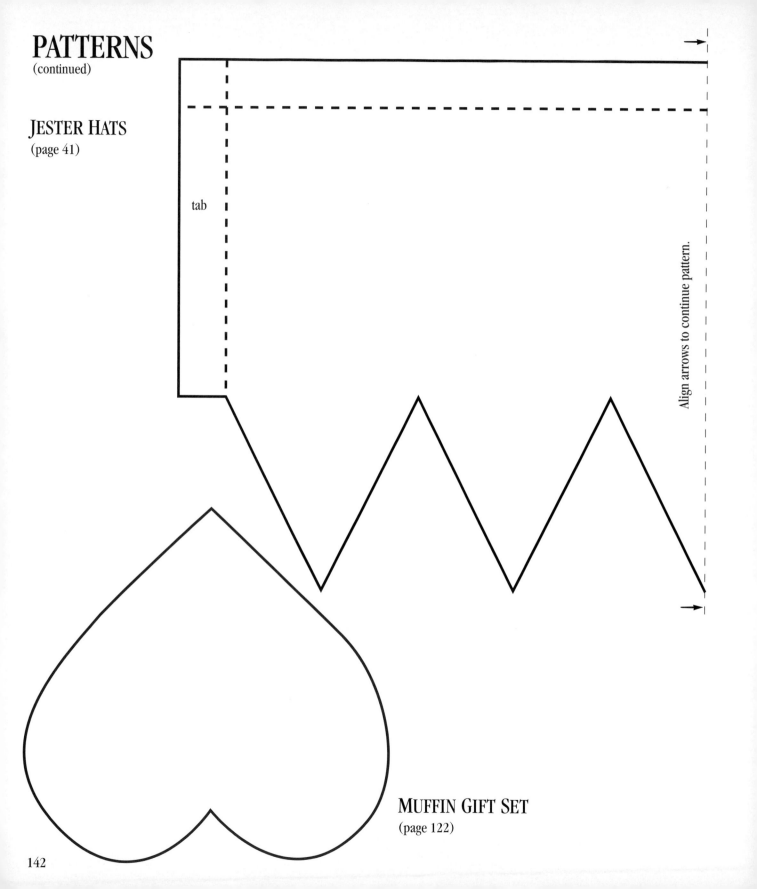

MUFFIN GIFT SET
(page 122)

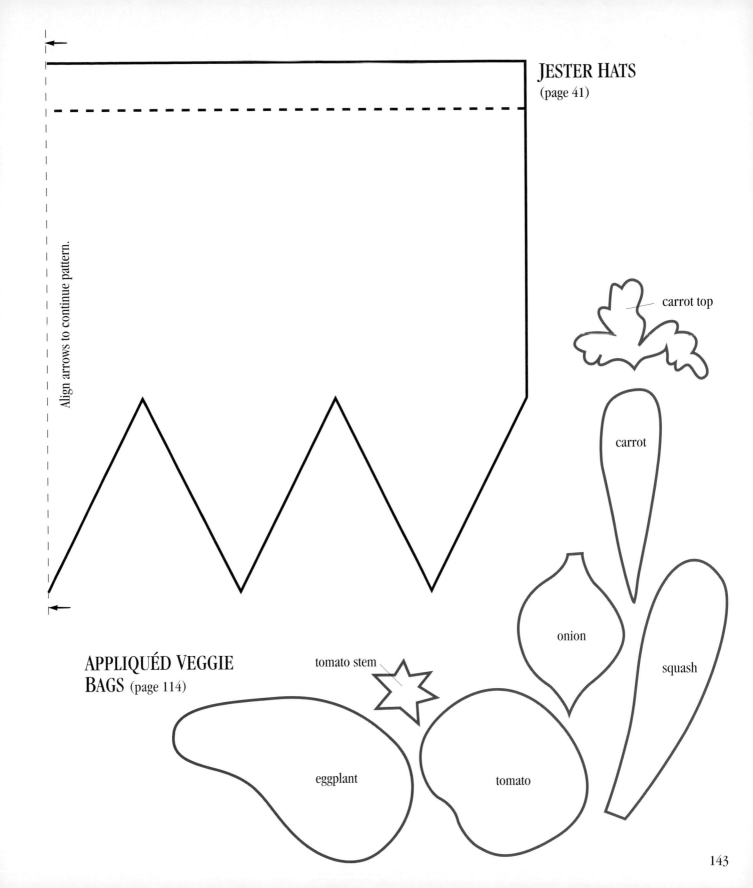

JESTER HATS
(page 41)

Align arrows to continue pattern.

carrot top

carrot

onion

squash

APPLIQUÉD VEGGIE BAGS (page 114)

tomato stem

eggplant

tomato

143

PATTERNS (continued)

"WELCOME, NEIGHBOR" PAN
(page 108)

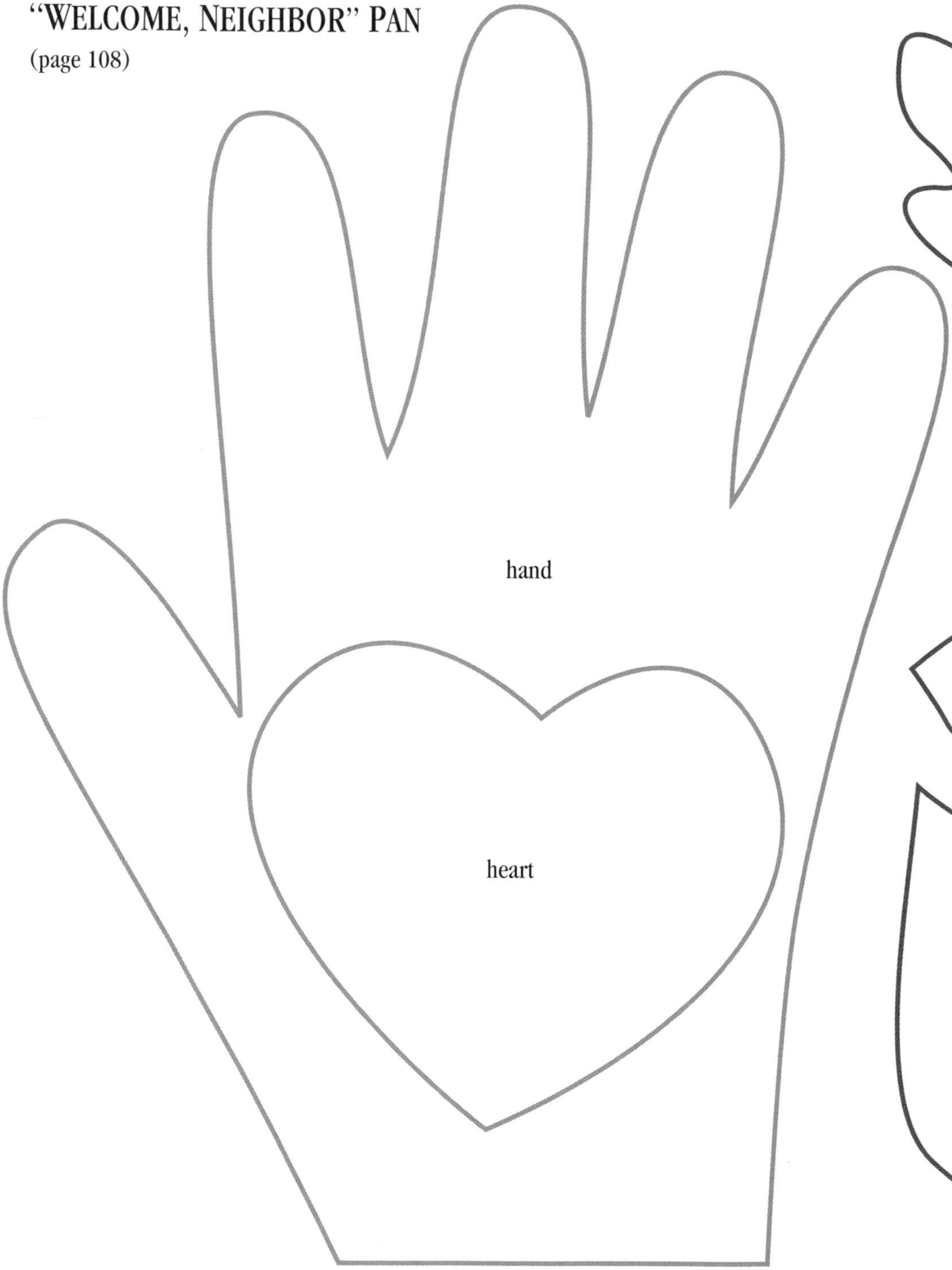

BREAD BASKET AND CLOTH
(page 118)

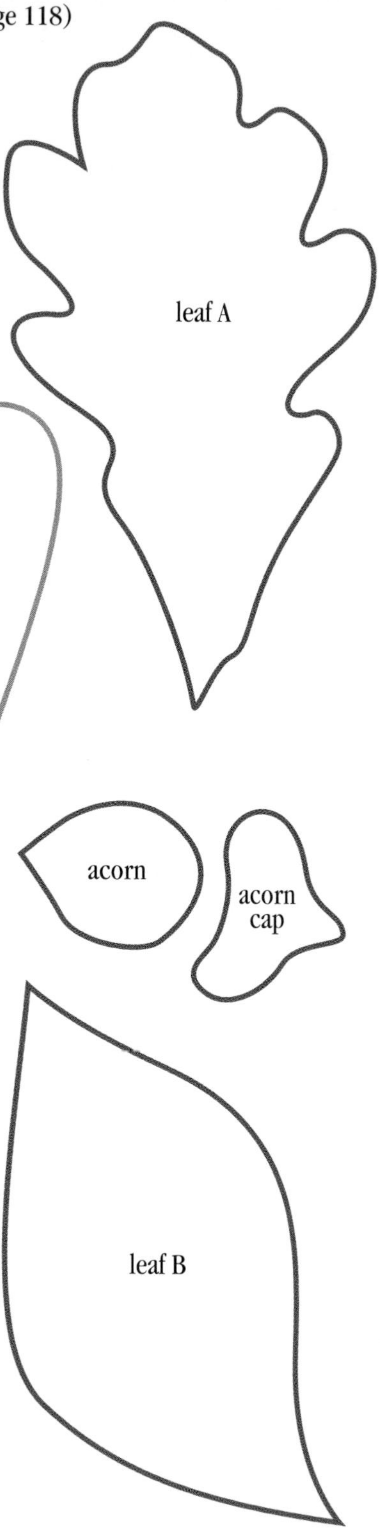

leaf A

hand

heart

acorn

acorn cap

leaf B

BREAD BASKET AND CLOTH
(page 118)

leaf D

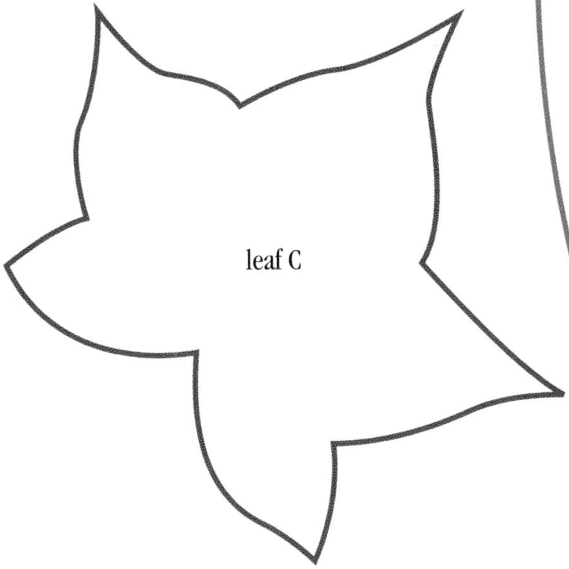

leaf C

HALLOWEEN GIFT BOX (page 129)

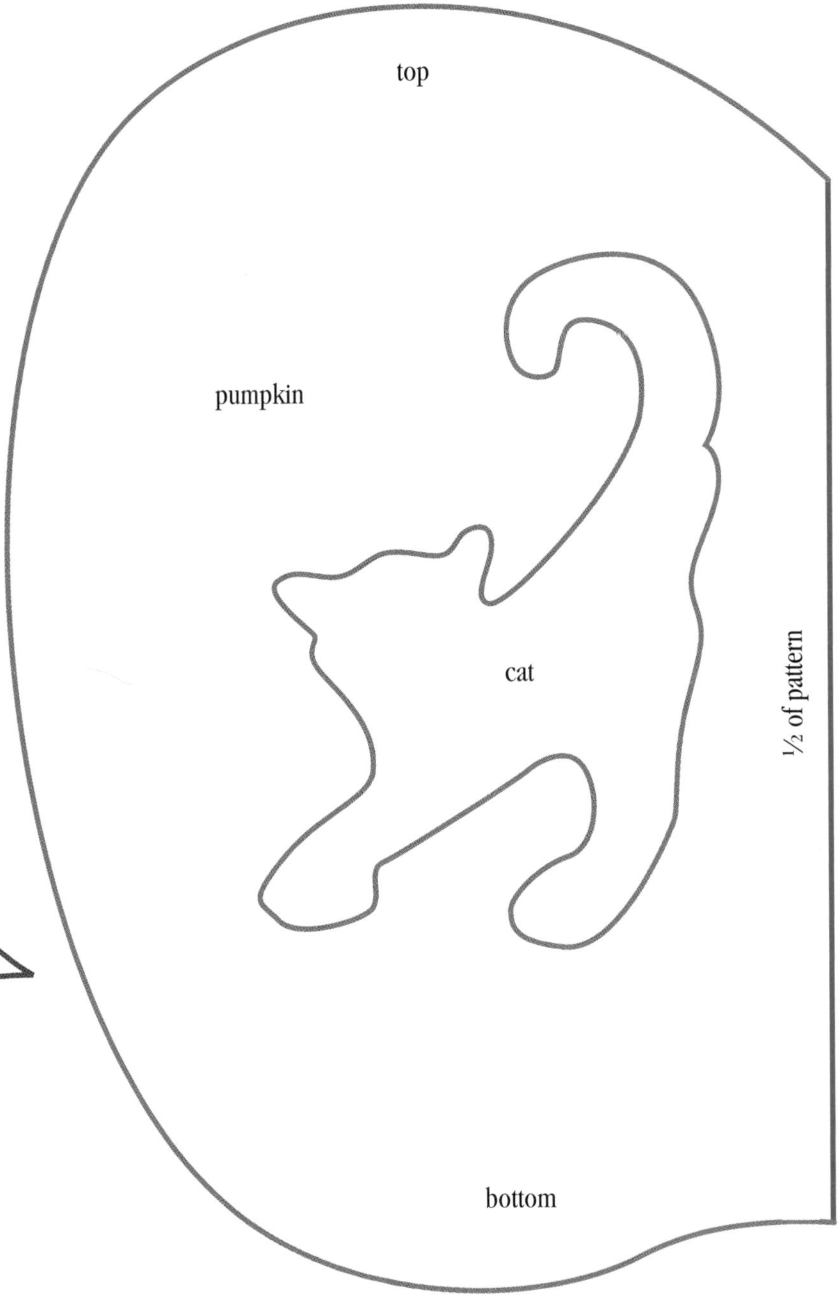

top

pumpkin

cat

bottom

½ of pattern

PATTERNS (continued)

Align arrows to continue pattern.

"RISE AND SHINE" CAKE PAN (page 121)

PATTERNS (continued)

TIE BOXES (page 105)

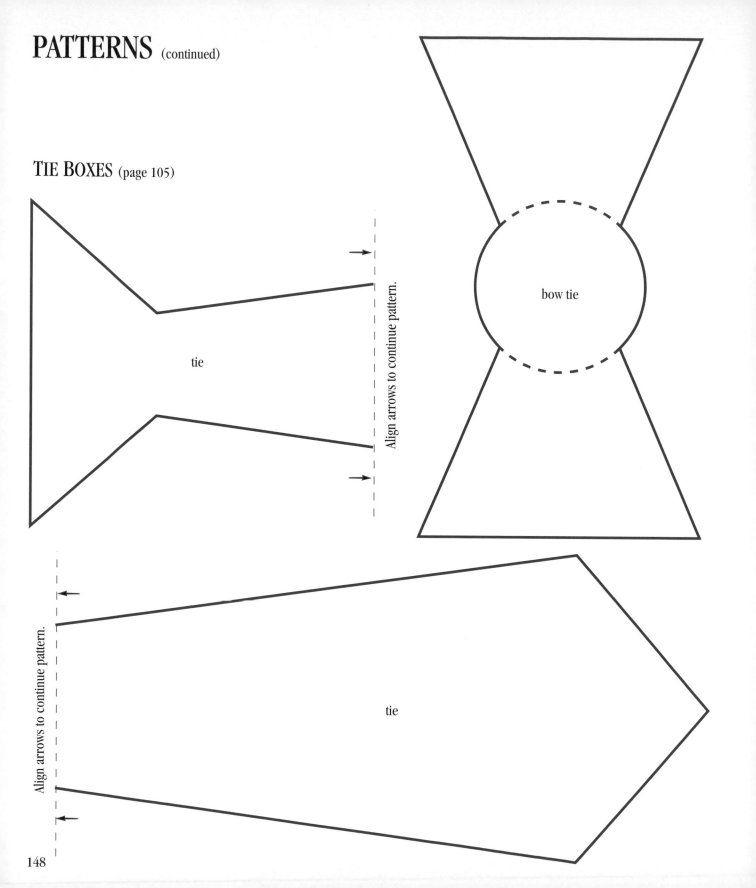

tie

Align arrows to continue pattern.

bow tie

Align arrows to continue pattern.

tie

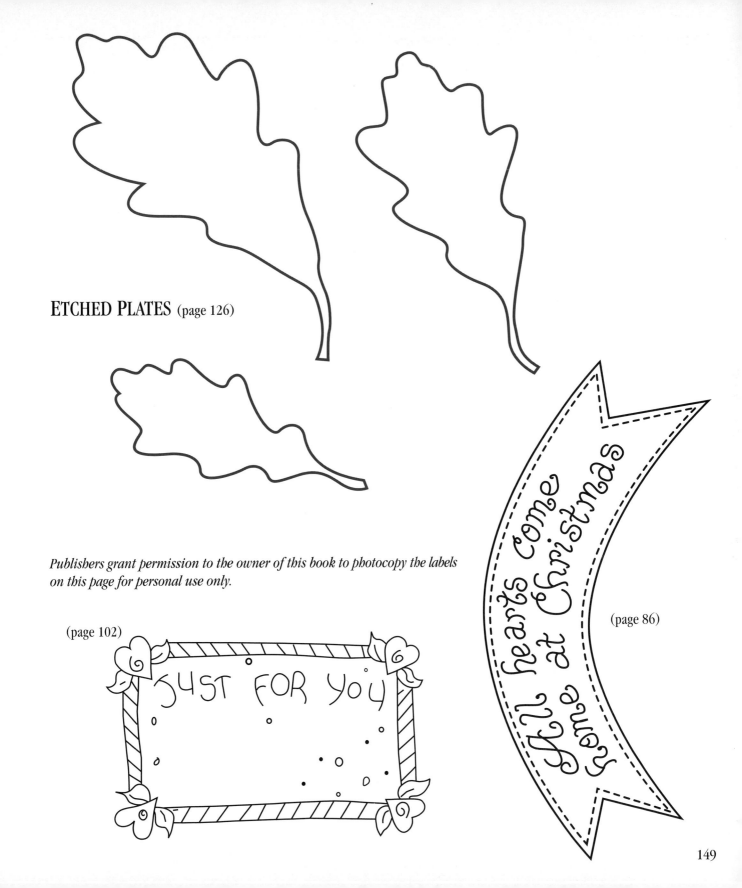

ETCHED PLATES (page 126)

Publishers grant permission to the owner of this book to photocopy the labels on this page for personal use only.

(page 102)

JUST FOR YOU

All hearts come home at Christmas

(page 86)

TO:
FROM:

(page 33)

(page 74)

Hope your Holidays are "delightful"

(page 56)

For the coffee lover!

(page 47)

to:
from:

(page 111)

(page 85)

To:

From:

MUST BE 21 TO EAT

(page 67)

pineapple

(page 73)

to:

from:

(pages 14 and 107)

(page 114)

GENERAL INSTRUCTIONS

ABOUT THE PAPER WE USED

For many of the projects in this book, we used white and colored paper. There are a variety of papers for these projects available at copy centers or crafts stores. When selecting paper, choose one that is suitable in weight for the project. We used copier paper, card and cover stock, construction paper, poster board, bristol board, and handmade paper.

ABOUT ADHESIVES

Refer to the following list when selecting adhesives. Carefully follow the manufacturer's instructions when applying adhesives.

CRAFT GLUE: Recommended for paper, fabric, wood, and floral items. Dry flat or secure with clothespins or straight pins until glue is dry.

FABRIC GLUE: Recommended for fabric or paper items. Dry flat or secure with clothespins or straight pins until glue is dry.

HOT- OR LOW-TEMPERATURE GLUE GUN AND GLUE STICKS: Recommended for paper, fabric, and floral items; hold in place until set. Dries quickly. Low-temperature glue does not hold as well as hot glue but offers a safer gluing option.

CRAFT GLUE STICK: Recommended for small, lightweight items. Dry flat.

SPRAY ADHESIVE: Recommended for adhering paper or fabric items. Dry flat.

RUBBER CEMENT: Recommended for adhering paper to paper; dries quickly.

DECOUPAGE GLUE: Recommended for applying fabric or paper pieces to smooth surfaces.

HOUSEHOLD CEMENT: Used for ceramic and metal items; secure until set.

COVERING A BOX

CAKE OR PIE BOX

1. Unfold box to be covered. Cut a piece of wrapping paper 1" larger on all sides than unfolded box. Place wrapping paper right side down on a flat surface.
2. For a small box, apply spray adhesive to outside of entire box. Center unfolded box, adhesive side down, on paper; press firmly to secure. For a large box, apply spray adhesive to bottom of box. Center unfolded box, adhesive side down, on paper; press firmly to secure. Applying spray adhesive to one section at a time, repeat to secure remaining sections of box to paper.
3. Place box on cutting mat and use a craft knife to cut paper even with edges of box. If box has slits, use craft knife to cut through slits from inside of box.
4. Reassemble box.

ASSEMBLED BOX

1. Cut a piece of paper large enough to cover box. Center box on wrong side of paper and draw around box.
2. Use ruler to draw lines 1/2" outside drawn lines, extending lines to edges of paper. Draw diagonal lines from intersections of outer lines to corners of original lines. Cut away corners of paper and clip along diagonal lines (Fig. 1).

Fig. 1

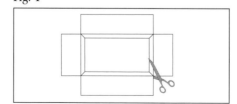

3. Apply spray adhesive to wrong side of paper.
4. Center box on paper, matching box to original drawn lines; smooth paper onto bottom of box.

5. Smooth paper onto front and back sides of box. Smooth excess paper around corners onto adjacent sides. Smooth paper to inside of box, clipping as necessary (Fig. 2).

Fig. 2

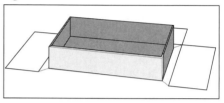

6. To cover each end, smooth paper onto end of box. Use craft knife and ruler to trim excess paper even with corners. Smooth paper to inside of box.

MAKING A BASKET LINER

For liner with an unfinished edge, cut or tear a fabric piece 1/4" larger on all sides than desired finished size of liner. Fringe edges of fabric piece 1/4" or use pinking shears to trim edges.

For liner with a finished edge, cut a fabric piece 1/2" larger on all sides than desired finished size of liner. Press edges of fabric piece 1/4" to wrong side; press 1/4" to wrong side again. Stitch in place.

MAKING PATTERNS

When entire pattern is shown, place tracing paper over pattern and trace pattern; cut out. For a more durable pattern, use a permanent pen to trace pattern onto stencil plastic; cut out.

When only half of pattern is shown (indicated by blue line on pattern), fold tracing paper in half and place fold along blue line of pattern. Trace pattern half. Turn folded paper over and draw over traced lines on remaining side of paper. Unfold paper and cut out pattern. For a more durable pattern, use a permanent pen to trace pattern half onto stencil plastic; turn stencil plastic over and align blue line with traced pattern half to form a whole pattern. Trace pattern half again; cut out.

When patterns are stacked or overlapped, place tracing paper over pattern and follow a single colored line to trace pattern. Repeat to trace each pattern separately onto tracing paper.

MAKING APPLIQUÉS

When tracing patterns for more than one appliqué, leave at least 1" between shapes on web.

To make a reverse appliqué, trace pattern onto tracing paper, turn traced pattern over, and follow all steps using traced pattern.

When an appliqué pattern contains shaded areas, trace along entire outer line for appliqué indicated in project instructions. Trace outer lines of shaded areas for additional appliqués indicated in project instructions.

1. Trace appliqué pattern onto paper side of web. (Some pieces may be given as measurements.) Cutting about 1/2" outside drawn lines, cut out web shape.
2. Follow manufacturer's instructions to fuse web shape to wrong side of fabric. Cut out shape along drawn lines.

MAKING A BOW

Loop sizes given in project instructions refer to the length of ribbon used to make one loop.

1. For first streamer, measure desired length of streamer from one end of ribbon; twist ribbon between fingers (Fig. 1).

Fig. 1

2. Keeping right side of ribbon facing out, fold ribbon to front to form desired-size loop; gather ribbon between fingers (Fig. 2). Fold ribbon to back to form another loop; gather ribbon between fingers (Fig. 3).

Fig. 2   Fig. 3

3. If a center loop is desired, form half the desired number of loops; then loosely wrap ribbon around thumb and gather ribbon between fingers (Fig. 4). Continue to form loops, varying size of loops as desired, until bow is desired size.

Fig. 4

4. For remaining streamer, trim ribbon to desired length.
5. To secure bow, hold gathered loops tightly. Fold a length of floral wire around gathers of loops. Hold wire ends behind bow, gathering all loops forward; twist bow to tighten wire. Arrange loops and trim ribbon ends as desired.

PAINTING TECHNIQUES

A disposable foam plate makes a good palette.

TRANSFERRING A PATTERN

Trace pattern onto tracing paper. Using removable tape, tape pattern to project. Place transfer paper, coated side down, between project and tracing paper. Use a pencil or an old ballpoint pen that does not write to transfer outlines of base coat areas of design to project. (Press lightly to avoid smudges and heavy lines that are difficult to cover.) If necessary, use a soft eraser to remove any smudges.

PAINTING BASE COATS

Use a medium round brush for large areas and a small round brush for small areas. Do not overload brush. Allowing to dry between coats, apply several thin coats of paint to project for adequate coverage.

TRANSFERRING DETAILS

To transfer detail lines to design, replace pattern and transfer paper over painted base coat; use pencil or old pen to lightly transfer detail lines onto project.

ADDING DETAILS

Use a permanent pen to draw over detail lines.

SPATTER PAINTING

Cover work area with paper and wear old clothes when spatter painting. Before painting item, practice painting technique on scrap paper.

continued on page 154

GENERAL INSTRUCTIONS (continued)

1. Place item on flat surface.
2. Mix 2 parts paint to 1 part water. Dip toothbrush in diluted paint and pull thumb firmly across bristles to spatter paint on item. Repeat as desired. Allow to dry.

SPONGE PAINTING

Use an assembly-line method when making several sponge-painted projects. Place project on a covered work surface. Practice sponge-painting technique on scrap paper until desired look is achieved. Paint projects with first color and allow to dry before moving to next color. Use a clean sponge for each additional color.

For allover designs, dip a dampened sponge piece into paint; remove excess paint on a paper towel. Use a light stamping motion to paint item.

For painting with sponge shapes, dip a dampened sponge shape into paint; remove excess paint on a paper towel. Lightly press sponge shape onto project. Carefully lift sponge. For a reverse design, turn sponge shape over.

MAKING A FABRIC BAG

Bag may be hand-stitched, machine-stitched, glued, or fused. Follow instructions below unless given specific measurements or different instructions in craft instructions.

1. To determine width of fabric needed, add ½" to desired finished width of bag. To determine length of fabric needed, double desired finished height of bag; add 1½". Cut a piece of fabric the determined measurements.
2. Matching right sides and short edges, fold fabric in half; finger press folded edge (bottom of bag). Using a ¼" seam allowance, sew sides of bag together.

3. For bag with flat bottom, match each side seam of fold line at bottom of bag; sew across each corner 2" from point (Fig. 1).

Fig. 1

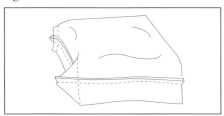

4. Press top edge of bag ¼" to wrong side; press again to ½" to wrong side and stitch in place.
5. Turn bag right side out.

CROSS STITCH

COUNTED CROSS STITCH (X)

Work one Cross Stitch for each colored square on chart. For horizontal rows, work stitches in two journeys (Fig. 1). For vertical rows, complete each stitch as shown in Fig. 2.

Fig. 1   Fig. 2

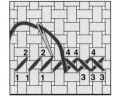

BACKSTITCH (B'ST)

For outline or details, Backstitch (shown in chart and color key by colored straight lines) should be worked after the design has been completed (Fig. 3).

Fig. 3

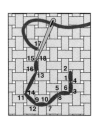

EMBROIDERY STITCHES

STRAIGHT STITCH

Insert needle up and down in garment as shown. Stitch length may be varied as desired.

Fig. 1

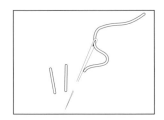

BLANKET STITCH

Knot one end of floss. Push needle up from wrong side of garment, even with edge of appliqué. Insert needle into appliqué and then come up at edge again, keeping floss below point of needle. Continue stitching in same manner, keeping stitches even (Fig. 2).

Fig. 2

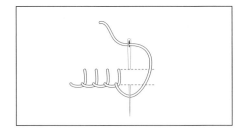

LAZY DAISY STITCH

Bring needle up at 1 and go down at 2 to form a loop; bring needle up at 3, keeping thread below point of needle (Fig. 1). Go down at 4 to anchor loop (Fig. 2).

Fig. 1   Fig. 2

RUNNING STITCH

Make a series of straight stitches with stitch length equal to the space between stitches (Fig. 3).

Fig. 3

RIBBON EMBROIDERY STITCHES

To retain the dimensional quality of silk ribbon, be careful not to pull it too tightly or twist it too much when stitching.

To thread needle, cut an approximate 14" length of ribbon. Thread one end of ribbon through eye of needle. Pierce same end of ribbon about 1/4" from end with point of needle (Fig. 1). Pull on remaining ribbon end, locking ribbon into eye of needle (Fig. 2).

Fig. 1

Fig. 2

To begin and end a length of ribbon, form a soft knot in ribbon by folding ribbon end about 1/4" and piercing needle through both layers (Fig. 3). Gently pull ribbon through to form a knot (Fig. 4). To end, secure ribbon on wrong side of fabric by tying a knot.

Fig. 3

Fig. 4

FRENCH KNOT

Bring needle up at 1. Wrap ribbon once around needle and insert needle at 2, holding ribbon with non-stitching fingers (Fig. 5). Tighten knot as close to fabric as possible while pulling needle back through fabric. For larger knot, use more lengths of ribbon; wrap only once.

Fig. 5

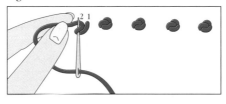

LAZY DAISY STITCH

Bring needle up at 1, take needle down again at 1 to form a loop, and bring needle up at 2, allowing ribbon to twist and keeping ribbon below point of needle (Fig. 6). Take needle down at 3 to anchor loop.

Fig. 6

JAPANESE RIBBON STITCH

Bring needle up at 1. Lay ribbon flat on fabric and take needle down at 2, piercing ribbon (Fig. 7). Gently pull needle through to back. Ribbon will curl at end of stitch as shown in Fig. 8.

Fig. 7

Fig. 8

SPIDERWEB ROSE

Use a removable fabric marking pen to lightly draw a circle the desired size of rose. For anchor stitches, use one strand of embroidery floss to work five straight stitches from edges of circle to center, bringing needle up at odd numbers and taking needle down at even numbers (Fig. 9). For ribbon petals, bring needle up at center of anchor stitches; weave ribbon over and under anchor stitches (Fig. 10), keeping ribbon loose and allowing ribbon to twist. Continue to weave ribbon until anchor stitches are covered. Take needle down to wrong side of fabric.

Fig. 9

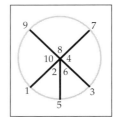

Fig. 10

KITCHEN TIPS

MEASURING INGREDIENTS

Liquid measuring cups have a rim above the measuring line to keep liquid ingredients from spilling. Nested measuring cups are used to measure dry ingredients, shortening, and peanut butter. Measuring spoons are used for measuring both dry and liquid ingredients.

To measure flour or granulated sugar: Spoon ingredient into nested measuring cup and level off with a knife. Do not pack down with spoon.

To measure confectioners sugar: Lightly spoon sugar into nested measuring cup and level off with a knife.

To measure brown sugar: Pack sugar into nested measuring cup and level off with a knife. Sugar should hold its shape when removed from cup.

To measure dry ingredients equaling less than 1/4 cup: Dip measuring spoon into ingredient and level off with a knife.

To measure shortening or peanut butter: Pack ingredient firmly into nested measuring cup and level off with a knife.

To measure liquids: Use a liquid measuring cup placed on a flat surface. Pour ingredient into cup and check measuring line at eye level.

To measure honey or syrup: For an accurate measurement, lightly spray measuring cup or spoon with vegetable oil cooking spray before measuring so that liquid will release easily from cup or spoon.

TESTS FOR CANDY MAKING

To determine the correct temperature of cooked candy, use a candy thermometer and the cold water test. Before each use, check the accuracy of your candy thermometer by attaching it to the side of a small saucepan of water, making sure thermometer does not touch bottom of pan. Bring water to a boil. Thermometer should register 212 degrees in boiling water. If it does not, adjust the temperature range for each candy consistency accordingly.

When using a candy thermometer, insert thermometer into candy mixture, making sure thermometer does not touch bottom of pan. Read temperature at eye level. Cook candy to desired temperature range. Working quickly, drop about 1/2 teaspoon of candy mixture into a cup of ice water. Use a fresh cup of water for each test. Use the following descriptions to determine if candy has reached the correct stage:

Soft-Ball Stage (234 to 240 degrees): Candy can be rolled into a soft ball in ice water but will flatten when removed from water.

Firm-Ball Stage (242 to 248 degrees): Candy can be rolled into a firm ball in ice water but will flatten if pressed when removed from water.

Hard-Ball Stage (250 to 268 degrees): Candy can be rolled into a hard ball in ice water and will remain hard when removed from water.

Soft-Crack Stage (270 to 290 degrees): Candy will form hard threads in ice water but will soften when removed from water.

Hard-Crack Stage (300 to 310 degrees): Candy will form brittle threads in ice water and will remain brittle when removed from water.

SOFTENING BUTTER OR MARGARINE

To soften 1 stick of butter, remove wrapper and place butter on a microwave-safe plate. Microwave on medium-low power (30%) 20 to 30 seconds.

SOFTENING CREAM CHEESE

To soften cream cheese, remove wrapper and place cream cheese on a microwave-safe plate. Microwave on medium power (50%) 1 to 1 1/2 minutes for an 8-ounce package or 30 to 45 seconds for a 3-ounce package.

SHREDDING CHEESE

To shred cheese easily, place wrapped cheese in freezer 10 to 20 minutes before shredding.

TOASTING NUTS

To toast nuts, spread nuts on an ungreased baking sheet. Stirring occasionally, bake in a 350-degree oven 5 to 8 minutes or until nuts are slightly darker in color.

PREPARING CITRUS FRUIT ZEST

To remove the zest (colored outer portion of peel) from citrus fruits, use a fine grater or citrus zester, being careful not to grate bitter white portion of peel.

TOASTING COCONUT

To toast coconut, spread a thin layer of coconut on an ungreased baking sheet. Stirring occasionally, bake in a 350-degree oven 5 to 7 minutes or until coconut is lightly browned.

MELTING CANDY COATING

To melt candy coating, place chopped coating in top of a double boiler over hot, not boiling, water or in a heavy saucepan over low heat. Stir occasionally with a dry spoon until coating melts. Remove from heat and use for dipping as desired. To flavor candy coating, add a small amount of flavored oil. To thin, add a small amount of vegetable oil, but no water. If necessary, coating may be returned to heat to remelt.

MELTING CHOCOLATE

To melt chocolate, place chopped chocolate in top of a double boiler over hot, not boiling, water or in a heavy saucepan over low heat. Stir occasionally with a dry spoon until chocolate melts. Remove from heat and use as desired. If necessary, chocolate may be returned to heat to remelt.

WHIPPING CREAM

For greatest volume, chill a glass bowl and beaters before beating whipping cream. In warm weather, place chilled bowl over ice while beating cream.

SUBSTITUTING HERBS

To substitute fresh herbs for dried, use 1 tablespoon fresh chopped herbs for 1 teaspoon dried herbs.

CUTTING OUT COOKIES

Place a piece of white paper or stencil plastic over pattern. Use a permanent felt-tip pen with fine point to trace pattern; cut out pattern. Place pattern on rolled-out dough and use a small sharp knife to cut out cookies. (*Note:* If dough is sticky, frequently dip knife into flour while cutting out cookies.)

EQUIVALENT MEASUREMENTS

1 tablespoon	=	3 teaspoons
$1/8$ cup (1 fluid ounce)	=	2 tablespoons
$1/4$ cup (2 fluid ounces)	=	4 tablespoons
$1/3$ cup	=	$5 1/3$ tablespoons
$1/2$ cup (4 fluid ounces)	=	8 tablespoons
$3/4$ cup (6 fluid ounces)	=	12 tablespoons
1 cup (8 fluid ounces)	=	16 tablespoons or $1/2$ pint
2 cups (16 fluid ounces)	=	1 pint
1 quart (32 fluid ounces)	=	2 pints
$1/2$ gallon (64 fluid ounces)	=	2 quarts
1 gallon (128 fluid ounces)	=	4 quarts

HELPFUL FOOD EQUIVALENTS

$1/2$ cup butter	=	1 stick butter
1 square baking chocolate	=	1 ounce chocolate
1 cup chocolate chips	=	6 ounces chocolate chips
$2 1/4$ cups packed brown sugar	=	1 pound brown sugar
$3 1/2$ cups unsifted confectioners sugar	=	1 pound confectioners sugar
2 cups granulated sugar	=	1 pound granulated sugar
4 cups all-purpose flour	=	1 pound all-purpose flour
1 cup shredded cheese	=	4 ounces cheese
3 cups sliced carrots	=	1 pound carrots
$1/2$ cup chopped celery	=	1 rib celery
$1/2$ cup chopped onion	=	1 small onion
1 cup chopped green pepper	=	1 large green pepper

RECIPE INDEX

CREDITS

To the talented people who helped in the creation of the following projects in this book, we extend a special word of thanks:

The Design Works Crafts, Inc.: *Cross-Stitched Santa Bag,* page 15.

Alisa Jane Hyde: *Sled Tray,* page 12; *Mitten Platter,* page 24; *Embellished Jars,* page 81; *Truffle Containers,* page 91; *Tie Boxes,* page 105; *Crate o' Barbecue Sauce,* page 106; *Bread Basket and Cloth,* page 118; *Etched Plates,* page 126.

Heidi King: *Napkin Rings and Matching Canisters,* page 70.

Laurie Knowles: *Cookie Jar,* page 64.

Deborah Lambein: *Angel Ornament Basket,* page 84.

Penny Lane Milligan: *Napkin Rings and Matching Canisters,* page 70; *Painted Tin,* page 72.

Amy Molloy: *Potato-Stamped Boxes,* page 26; *Tote Bag and Covered Jar,* page 40; *Sleigh Packaging,* page 45; *Painted Jar,* page 52; *Pie Stand and Server,* page 54; *Aromatic Coasters and Matching Tin,* page 82; *Beaded Fruit Jar,* page 90; *Oven Mitt Packaging,* page 120; *Serving Tray,* 123.

Pamela Nissen: *Bread and Basket Wrapping,* page 42.

Dondra G. Parham: *Jester Hats,* page 41.

Carol Tipton: *Snowmen Mugs,* page 16; *Fabric-Covered Gift Box and Gift Tag,* page 18; *Christmas Lights Cake Cover,* page 36; *Gingerbread Man Dish Towel,* page 38; *Jester Hats,* page 41; *Peppermint Jars,* page 44; *Chiffon Cake Box,* page 49; *Candy Christmas Tree,* page 77; *Painted Tray,* page 80; *Mardi Gras Bags,* page 96; *Easter Egg Box,* page 98; *Wreath Pie Server,* page 127; *Autumn Boxes,* page 130.

Patricia Weaver: *Cutout Christmas Box,* page 21; *Fruited Carafes,* page 28; *Embellished Bottle,* page 29; *Cookie Containers,* page 37; *Dessert Glasses and Matching Jars,* page 46; *Decorated Bucket,* page 51; *Bauble Cake Plate,* page 57; *Jar and Honey Dipper,* page 65.

Becky Werle: *Santa Lollipop Cookies,* page 43; *Snowman Cookies,* page 71.

Cynthia Moody Wheeler: *Leaf-Imprinted Bread Basket Cloth,* page 22; *Candy Cane Bag,* page 34; *Candy Cane Jar,* page 66.

Madeline White: *Leaf-Imprinted Bread Basket Cloth,* page 22; *Beaded Ice Cream Scoop and Jar,* page 25.